Maurice Baren

DEDICATION

After our wedding over 35 years ago, Judith and I made our first home in one of the cottages in the grounds of Towneley Hall in Burnley. Neither of us came from Lancashire, but the members and friends of Towneley Methodist Church made us so welcome and that friendship has lasted long after we left the county. This book is dedicated, with thanks, to them.

AUTHOR'S NOTE

Many people have helped this book, my seventh, to come into being and I am very grateful for all the support I have received. Firstly I must thank the companies that are featured in the book and the aid that owners, their staff and retired members gave me, either by books, reminiscences or illustrations. The staff at several Local Study libraries also were most helpful, including those at Clitheroe, Burnley, Morecambe, Southport, Liverpool, Bury and Manchester — many thanks for your time and co-operation. Many individual people have helped in a variety of ways and I would like to particularly thank Tom and Peggy Hewitt, Dr Fred Kidd, Mr Morton, Duncan Stevenson, Robert Baxter, Andrew Berry, David Cam, Philip Swindells, Geoff and Margaret Race, N B Redman, Mary Pedlar, Jim Reid, Philip Byrne, Mary and Tony Sinacola, Gillian Lonergan, Sue Holden, Cliff Cowburn, Peter Rodwell, Neil Kenyon, Tony Duerr, Adrian Figgess, Leslie Plommer, Horace Halewood, Gillian Robson, Jonathan Barr, Shami Ahmed, Lisa Huxter, Gordon Baron, John Hutchinson, Paul Isherwood, Neil Lloyd, W (Bill) Oddie, Arthur Morley, Chris Moore, Steve Waring, Adam Gentilli, John Hartwright, S Tew, John Winnard, Margaret Booth, Eric Ogden, Bert Shearing, Mark Collinge, John Timpson, and Sue Nichols, Lesley Owen-Edwards, Jim Robinson, Frank Weighill, Frank Neville, Prof T C Barker, Chris Redman, Mark Page, The Lancashire Museum, Unilever Historical Archives, Liverpool Record Office (bottom picture page 9), Lancashire Evening Telegraph (picture page 47) and Bury Times Newspaper (picture page 49).

The Dalesman Publishing Company are always a pleasure to work with and I would particularly like to thank general manager Robert Flanagan, designer Barbara Allen and Rachel Allen who looks after marketing and sales — a most important concern of any author!

Eric Knowles (Mr Burnley!) so readily agreed to write the Foreword — it really was much appreciated and his is a valuable contribution to the work.

Finally but certainly not least, I want to thank my wife Judith who increasingly helps with the research, but is also an encourager and support in times of despair, as well as sharing my joy when we make a significant discovery.

I do apologise if I have left anyone out who feels their contribution should have been mentioned; it is difficult to remember all contacts. However, any such omissions will be remedied in a future edition if the person concerned cares to contact me or my publisher.

CONTENTS

FOREWORD

As both my parents and grandparents queued at the bacon counter of Redman's, bought their oven bottom cakes at Oddies and drank gallons of Vimto, hot in winter and cold in summer, Maurice Baren decided that I obviously possessed the necessary credentials to offer this foreword. Having been born in the shadow of Pendle Hill in what is still known as "Witch Country", I readily admit to a reluctance to eulogise about my birth place, if only to avoid the onslaught of tourists.

Being born a Lancastrian was a stroke of good fortune although my town of Nelson was little more than a few miles from the Yorkshire border and some might consider it "a near run thing".

At the time of writing, my life can be seen to consist of two distinct periods. The first consigned to my birth and formative years in the county of the red rose and the latter to carving out a career "down in the smoke".

History has always proved an irresistible fascination to me ever since I was taken as a small boy to nearby Towneley Hall in Burnley. Since that time my thirst for knowledge has grown, and now that I have read this intriguing book I feel better armed to face both Northern and Southern tribes whether lecturing or broadcasting.

I am without question a better person for knowing the beginnings of Uncle Joe's Mint Balls, without forgetting Messrs Holland, purveyors to the great British public of the finest meat pies and steak puddings.

How It All Began In Lancashire offers a showcase of what may be considered as the best of what Lancashire has and continues to offer. Those who live or have lived in the county Palatine recognise that there is even more that could have been included and hopefully we can look forward to How It All Began In Lancashire, Volume Two.

ERIC KNOWLES

INTRODUCTION

There has always been conflict between the county of the Red Rose and the one that takes as its emblem the White Rose. Whilst I may be a Yorkshireman I lived in Lancashire for four happy years and frequently make the journey across the Pennines. As with my book How It All Began in Yorkshire, I have again taken the historic county boundary rather than the modern local government boundaries.

Lancashire has been the birthplace of many inventions, or its people have taken the germ of an idea and developed it into something of significant benefit to many people – commercial television in Manchester, the Co-operative movement at Rochdale, the motor industry at Leyland, glass at St Helens, or the Mersey Tunnel in Liverpool to name just a few.

As the economic structure of the country has changed, so Lancashire's industry has had to respond to those changes, often at great personal sacrifice by its various workforces. However, today we see a county that still has some long established businesses as well as modern hi-tech concerns. For many years Liverpool was a major port, its ships reaching out across the world; today Lancashire is at the centre of transportation – motorways pass through the county, its canals form an important contribution to the carriage of goods and the tourist industry, whilst Manchester Airport is one of Britain's busiest bringing and taking people to all parts of the world.

This has been a fascinating book to research and I hope, you the reader, will enjoy reading the stories we have discovered, and perhaps seeing again some of the old advertisements and other ephemera which touch your memory.

MAURICE BAREN

BIBLIOGRAPHY

Sidney Berstein – A Biography by Caroline Moorhead (Cape 1984)

Here we Were by Gordon Winter, Golden Jubilee of Granada Group of Companies

The History of the Boddingtons Brewery by N B Redman, Archivist Whitbread PLC

The Story of Blackpool Rock by Margaret Race

Booths – 150 Years of Progress (published 1997)

Vimto – The story of a Soft Drink by Sue Nichols (Carnegie Publishing 1994)

C P Scott 1846-1932 The Making of the Manchester Guardian (F Muller 1946)

Manchester Ship Canal Centenary Programme 1894 - 1994

Brooke Bond – a hundred years by David Wainwright

Close-Up – Manchester Airport

First and Foremost (a history of Manchester Airport) by Alan Scholefield

Hartley – The Life of Sir William Hartley by Arthur S. Peake, DD

BRITANNIA
ADELPHI
HOTEL

Tens of thousands of people will feel they know the Adelphi Hotel from having watched the story of its daily life in the television series which became prime-time viewing, but it has been welcoming guests to the port and to the city for over 150 years!

In 1826, Copperas Hill, on which the Adelphi Hotel now stands, consisted of a row of houses which were built in 1790. Its frontage in Ranelagh Place, looking down Ranelagh Street, and also near to the site of the yet to be developed Central (Lime Street) Railway Station, gave it a commanding position over the city. About 1826 two of these houses were bought by William and Joseph Ewart, who converted them into the Adelphi Hotel. Almost immediately it passed into the ownership of James Radley, and in 1868 it was enlarged and its accommodation more than doubled. As early as 1872, in the Hotel Guide to Liverpool, the Adelphi Hotel is described as being 'before all its competitors in the elements of luxuriance, comfort and ele-

From modest beginnings in the early 1830s (below) to star of its own TV series (above), the Adelphi has been welcoming visitors through its doors for over 150 years.

gance'. Picton's Memorials of Liverpool, first printed in 1875, tells us that Radley gradually bought every house in the row until the entire block became part of the Adelphi Hotel. Radley had previously been a hotelier in London, and with this previous experience, his charm, enthusiasm and great ability, he made the Adelphi Hotel the most popular in Liverpool, and very

quickly it became well-known throughout Britain and Europe.

The Adelphi Hotel was the first resting place of new United States Ambassadors to the Court of St James, and here they would receive addresses of welcome from the Mayor and Corporation. Later in the 1920s, when Liverpool was a bustling port, scores of liveried porters would move mounds of cabin trunks and other luggage as the rich and the famous crossed the Adelphi's threshold; one can also visualise the magnificent cars which they arrived in. There were also the stars from the Empire Theatre and those involved in, or attending, such events as the Aintree Grand National – many a priceless autograph has been gained on the steps of the Adelphi!

The layout of its numerous rooms gave it the privacy of a home, being shaped round an inner quadrangle. In the basement of this quadrangle were the wine cellars, the pantries, the ice house, sleeping accommodation for some of the staff and an immense laundry. Rather more unusual was a tank where 60 or 70 turtles swam comfortably – unaware that the chef would be using them shortly as part of his culinary delights; indeed The Adelphi had a reputation for its turtle soup!

On the ground floor the kitchen was so cut off from the main rooms that no hint of cooking smells pervaded the atmosphere. On this floor was also the large smoking and reading room, not only well supplied with newspapers and magazines but where telegrams were delivered from all parts of the world – perhaps telling of that day's changes in the New York Gold Market or the price of cotton in Bombay. Also on this floor was the magnificent coffee and dining room, and attached to it a billiard room with six tables and its own bar. For ladies and families there were apartments which were en suite, with drawing-room, bedroom and bathroom, again ensuring complete privacy, but also there was a ladies' dining-room, writing-room and drawing room.

To the rear of the building were special suites provided exclusively for members of the Masonic bodies. Finally there was a splendid reception room leading by a separate staircase to the great banqueting hall and ballroom on the first floor. The hotel at that time had 200 bedrooms and 22 sitting-rooms with accommodation for about 300 guests.

On Radley's death in 1863, the hotel was regarded as one of the most valuable hotel properties in the country and was sold to a joint stock company who also carried out many improvements, but it wasn't until 1912 that it reached its zenith.

In 1912 Arthur Towle, one of Britain's great hoteliers, believed that Liverpool needed a hotel of the stature of the Midland Hotel in Manchester (following a tour of the great hotels of Europe and America he had helped in its design and construction) and he acquired and rebuilt the Adelphi.

The building we see today has changed little from that which he opened in 1913 – inside there are solid marble walls on the upper levels, a fine indoor heated swimming pool, sauna baths, and it was the first hotel in Liverpool to have central heating in all rooms. The Sefton Suite was created as a replica of the First Class Smoking Lounge on the Titanic.

It was a tremendous undertaking and involved huge capital outlay, but the shareholders were generally wealthy men and were more concerned with its quality and prestige. The Adelphi flourished, not least as a first taste of Britain for those arriving on the great liners which had crossed the Atlantic from America and other parts of the world.

Over the intervening years the Adelphi Hotel has known good years, but also times of

In its heyday the Adelphi ranked among the world's finest luxury hotels with decor and fittings based upon the style of a luxury liner

neglect. Many years ago Roy Rogers and his faithful horse Trigger made a grand entrance from the Mezzanine floor, down the stairs to the Main Lounge, where he was greeted by an enormous audience.

In 1929 there was a great need to encourage people to have confidence in Liverpool, to enable it to come out of industrial decline, and one evening Lord Woolton held a dinner-party at the Adelphi to which he invited the Lord Mayor and the chairman of the Finance Committee. His aim was to persuade them to incorporate the rural district of Speke into the city, and build an aerodrome there – it was a decision which put Liverpool among those cities which had their own airport.

In later years the hotel became a venue for pop groups, film stars and television personalities, but by 1984 it was a very weary, tired place. Owned by British Transport Hotels, a subsidiary of British Rail, its top two floors were closed in a bid to save on rates, and pigeons and rain led to even more decay and ruin.

Shortly before the hotel was to close its doors for the last time, it was purchased by the Britannia Hotel Group, and became the Britannia Adelphi Hotel. As part of a total refurbishment the two top floors were made into single and club rooms, whilst the bedrooms on the first four floors were restored to their former splendour. Additional bedrooms have now been added at the rear of the hotel, giving a total of 402 bedrooms. Public areas and function rooms have also been renewed with contemporary fittings and exquisite chandeliers. Today Liverpool can once again be proud of the Adelphi Hotel which has served its visitors and townspeople so well.

After varying fortunes the Grand Style is once again the order of the day at the hotel where visitors can dine in the splendour of the Derby Room (above) with food prepared by Executive Chef David H Smith

On a busy Saturday it is possible to find the hotel acting as host to no less than seven wedding parties; it is also a regular venue for important conferences, but to the family party or business group it also offers friendliness with efficiency.

To many people it will always remain that hotel seen on the 'telly', with Eileen Downey very much in charge – but for others the Adelphi will be a place of splendour, a place where memories were made. It is as much a part of the heritage of Liverpool as its people, its waterfront or its industry, but it also lives on to serve the future, offering hospitality and care as it has done for over a century and a half.

JAMES BAXTER & SON EST 1799

The Baxter family have been in Morecambe since about 1640; then they were fishermen, today they are renowned for their potted shrimps. Bob Baxter is the sixth generation of men, and women, who have gained their livelihood from the 'harvest of the sea'. Their company dates from 1799.

The family have potted shrimps since about 1880, but in the late part of the 19th century Bob's grandfather, another James Baxter, married Margaret Wright who came from Marshside near Southport, where 'shrimping' was a more common occupation.

Margaret opened a shop in Morecambe to sell 'wet' fish, and lived over the shop; later they bought a house on the Promenade and opened a café. She has been described as a 'formidable woman from Southport' and 'the pioneer of potted shrimps'! The family used to have a fleet of fishing boats, expanded their 'wet' fish shops and ran a chain of restaurants. The main one served 2000 meals a day. At one time the company also made shrimp and lobster paste.

In the 1920s two brothers, Walter and Percy, formed Morecambe Trawlers Ltd, a co-operative, but grandfather James did not become part of it. Walter said the business would fulfil a long-felt want, which earned him the nickname 'Long-Felt Want' – many fishermen had nicknames at this time! The co-operative closed down in 1989 when the number of boats fishing in the bay had reduced to six.

Morecambe's decline as a holiday resort, particularly for day-trippers, became most obvious in the 1960s and following the death of his father Harry Baxter, Bob decided to dispose of several of the businesses to concentrate on frozen food and shrimps. At this time he took over £10,000 per week in wholesale and retail sales of frozen goods. However, as supermarkets came to the town he saw this market reduce dramatically. Morecambe declined as a shopping centre in 1990 when Marks & Spencer closed their store. By 1995 Bob had made his business much smaller, concentrating on the potted shrimps for which the company was granted a Royal Warrant in the 1960s, first from the Queen Mother, and later from Her Majesty The Queen.

Harry Baxter in his van and, below, Baxter's café in Queen Street in Morecambe

The shrimp used in 'potting' is a diminutive brown scavenger, 1^{1}/$_{2}$-2" long, turning shiny brown when boiled. It is found in sandy inshore waters, often 3-4 miles from the shore and at a depth of about 30 fathoms, in an area stretching from the Solway Firth to the Dee. The shrimps are most plentiful in spring and autumn and are caught from boats.

In the early 1920s there were about 100 of the 30-35 foot 'Nobby' boats involved in the industry; now there are very few. Today fishermen have much smaller families and few follow their father into the business. The men had to be up at 3am to go and catch the shrimps and spent many hours at sea. An average catch would be 10-20 stone, but this might double during September and October. The women also helped by making sails for the fishing boats, using old treadle sewing machines, or by knitting fish nets. Shrimps, nocturnal creatures which bury themselves in the sand during daylight hours, are sometimes known as 'The King of Morecambe Bay' and a 1990 survey concluded that they were free from bacteria and viruses. Baxter's use eight professional fishermen to catch their shrimps, some of whose families have been working with them for four generations.

The catch is cleaned and graded (the small ones being thrown back into the sea) then boiled in sea water on the fishing boat. In the

Change on the menu: an early advert during the years of the First World War and a modern product shot show how the marketing of Baxter's shrimps has changed

past the families of the fishermen, mainly wives and daughters, peeled the shrimps with their fingers, often being referred to locally as 'pickers'. However, it is hard work, and the number of women prepared to do it has declined.

On coming to Baxter's the shrimps are stewed in best butter and spices, no preservatives being added, spread on trays to cool, turned and folded to evenly distribute the juices, and when cold, women deftly press them into cartons.

The importance of shrimps to the business increased in the 1960s and its growth in mail order came in the early 1990s. Everything is done as it always has been, including the hand packing into plastic cartons, which are now used instead of the original pots. Some women became very skilful at 'potting'; indeed, it was reported that two women could fill 500 pots a day. Today Baxter's has a staff of six people, four of whom are involved in production. All have had a long involvement with the company.

Today, Bob Baxter, who has spent 52 years in the fishing industry, along with his dedicated team, supply 3,000 mail order customers. The list of customers includes royalty and many titled people, as well as high class shops and restaurants in various parts of the British Isles.

HJ BERRY & SONS

The little village of Chipping, between Preston and Clitheroe, already had a thriving cottage industry of chair-making at the beginning of the 19th century; there was fine wood to be found locally in the Forest of Bowland. However, the name Chipping has no connection with the chair-making industry, but is derived from the old English name for a market place. John Berry, the founder of the company, was born in 1835 at Dutton near Ribchester, the eldest son of farmer James and

John Berry, the company founder

his wife Agnes. James and Agnes moved to Buckley Hall, Ribchester, but James died when John was only nine and he, his mother and the four other young children returned to live at Dutton. The village had woods which provided timber for the local craftsmen. In 1858, when he married Martha Watson, John Berry described himself as a carpenter, although in those days that could include tree-felling, coffin making or

house repairing. After the wedding John and Martha moved to Chipping, where they spent the rest of their lives, and where many people were employed in small chair-making businesses.

Chipping was a thriving village and the young couple went to live at 'The Folly', a stone cottage just off the Chipping to Longridge Road. John worked at Stump Mill where he probably had just a small section for his business. It wasn't until 1866 that the couple had a son, Henry James, although they had seven daughters. Perhaps due to the large family they found it helpful to move to Grove Row to live, for money must have been tight, and John started to use a disused chapel at Bottoms.

The decline of the cotton industry brought many changes to Chipping, and not always prosperity. However, the increasing number of people involved in chair-making led to amalgamations rather than competition. By now Martha Jane, John's sister, had married John Seed and it is likely that he worked with John at Tweedy's Foundry, where his father-in-law produced simple farmhouse chairs and stools, and which was about half a mile up the road from the present works. The cottage industry had become a factory based business.

Berry's "Rush Bottomers" photographed (top) at the Royal Lancashire Show, circa 1900, and (below) the Rush Bottomer today

Where it all began – the village of Chipping

UTILITY DINING CHAIRS

No. 708. Mahogany
709. Oak

No. 712. Mahogany
713. Oak

No. 715. Oak

H. J. BERRY & SONS LIMITED, KIRK MILLS, CHIPPING, LANCS.

Chairmakers Since 1840

The enterprise succeeded and in 1880 needed a new home. Kirk Mills, a local cotton mill built in 1785 to house over a thousand Arkwright water-powered spinning frames, was taken over by John's son, Henry James Berry, after whom the present company is named. These premises are still used by the company, and its original thirty-six foot diameter water wheel, which powered wood-working machinery until 1942, is still in place.

In those early days Henry boasted that the company could turn its hand to any kind of furniture – 'from cradle to coffin', but also from chair to pig trough if necessary, always being careful not to turn away an order whether it came from some fine hall or a local farm. Indeed, in summer work would often be suspended so that the men could help with haymaking; cows and other animals were kept in Kirk Mills yard, and even up to World War Two milking was a feature of the working day. The company also made good use of horse drawn transport until 1942.

In the 1890s John Berry lost one of his arms in a sawmill accident but this did not prevent him working as hard as two men. Even on his retirement he took on a new job – that of landlord at the Sun Inn. From there John provided refreshments and loaned the Sun Inn Meadows for the village's celebrations for Queen Victoria's Diamond Jubilee in 1897.

Utility furniture produced during the Second World War, Nineties catalogue cover and child's school chair

In 1902 the company purchased Kirk Mill factory for £2,355; at that time production was only about a dozen chairs a day.

By 1920 the number of workers had risen to twenty and they worked a 55 hour week, from 6am to 5pm! Electricity was late in coming to Chipping – it didn't arrive until 1923, and then it came courtesy of H J Berry & Sons. An article, a decade later, tells us that production had now risen to 200 chairs a day, and individual workers now had to specialise in their part of the production.

Henry James Berry died in 1940, aged 74, and was succeeded by his elder son, John, who during the 1940s won substantial orders for NAAFI and children's

furniture and this enabled them to maintain full production during those difficult years. In 1942 John's brother died in a tragic accident in the swollen Chipping Brook. In 1947 H J Berry & Sons became a limited company and the new mill was built; since then a large chair store and timber shed have also been added. After the war the company started to manufacture utility furniture and with new equipment were able to kiln-dry timber.

In 1966, at the age of 70, John Berry died. He had been a notable local figure and his funeral was attended by about 500 people. His life is commemorated in an attractive stained glass window in the village church, pictured left. The current managing director, Jack Berry, was awarded the MBE in 1999 for his services to the local community.

Today the staff at Berry's control production from the receipt of raw logs, their sawing into planking, stacking for seasoning (which can take up to three years) and then the kiln-drying to reduce the moisture content to the optimum level for indoor use. From taking the original log to producing the finished piece of furniture there is an amazing 50 per cent wastage – which is not quite true when you consider that offcuts and sawdust go to heat the kilns or the works. The timbers used are all British hardwoods and some of the seats are made of traditional materials such as rushes – a 'rush-bottomed' seat can take a local craftsman three hours to complete, using only the finest bullrushes.

As well as producing chairs for furnishing homes, many of the pieces of furniture produced at Chipping are developed for specialist uses such as in the health care service where it is essential that some chairs should have reinforced arms or special wheels which enable them to glide over a variety of surfaces. Other ranges have been developed for contract furnishing of hotels, offices and churches.

Today the fifth generation take the same pride in ensuring the quality of their products as those cottage industry friends did 150 years ago – only today they no longer make pig troughs or do the milking!

Stacking chairs are now a Berry's speciality

Blackpool was first connected by rail to the industrial towns of East Lancashire in 1846, but it wasn't until the last decade of that century that the working classes started coming to the seaside resort in large numbers. In August 1903 it was estimated that as many as a quarter of a million people slept in Blackpool over the August Bank Holiday weekend.

Such crowds needed entertainment – in Paris the Eiffel Tower was built for the Paris Exposition of 1889, and Blackpool opened its Tower in 1894.

The Tower offered a range of buildings at its base, including a circus, an aquarium and a magnificent ballroom. Blackpool also had its North and South Piers, its Grand Theatre, as well as the Winter Gardens with its Empress Ballroom. A company was also formed to erect the 220 foot Great Wheel. All these developments cost vast sums of money and some of the companies collapsed, bringing an end to such large scale endeavours.

Meanwhile, down on the sand-dunes at the south of the town gypsies made a living by telling

The Pleasure Beach as captured at night by Lord Lichfield in 1989 and, below, the sand hills of South Shore at the end of the 19th century before it all began. The Star Inn is on the right, the sea beyond.

fortunes and operating an early switchback. Another newcomer was John Outhwaite from Yorkshire who set up 'Outhwaite's American Merry-go-round' – a gift from his father-in-law in Philadelphia, where he manufactured the roundabouts. Nearby, William George Bean, who was born in Chelsea in 1868, leased a site beside the gypsy encampment. William, after a time in advertising, had been to Philadelphia where he had got involved in the amusement industry, but in 1895 he returned to England with the sole rights to operate the Bicycle Railway.

Early in the new century William Bean joined forces with John Outhwaite, and with a £30,000 mortgage from the Royal Liverpool Friendly Society they bought the 'Watson's Estate', about 30 acres of sand hills along the shore line, and other rough ground further inland. As other developments took place along the seafront the Borough Council started to restrict and control such activities but William Bean, wanting also to create a good quality amusement park, met all its demands. He encouraged other people to form companies to operate further American 'devices' in his fairground. Among them was Sir Hiram S Maxim, who built his Flying Machine, which is still in operation today some 90 years later!

By 1905 Blackpool had its 'Pleasure Beach'! Also during that year a Helter Skelter Lighthouse was erected, a beacon to guide people to the Pleasure Beach. Other spectacular rides followed including a Dark Water Ride, River Caves of the World, and in 1907 the ever popular Water Chute. In 1908 the Canadian Toboggan Slide opened and the following year a Roller Skating rink was added.

In 1907 William Bean became a town councillor and in 1910 Blackpool Pleasure Beach Ltd was formed with him as Chairman and Managing Director. John Outhwaite died suddenly in 1911, and although his family inherited his share of the business, they sold their share to Bean's successor in 1931.

More and more attractions arrived – in 1910 the Joy Wheel, 1911 the Bowl Slide, and in 1912 the world's first Rainbow Wheel. In 1913, at a cost of £13,352, the Casino was built on the

promenade, at the approach to the Pleasure Beach – the name originally meant a pavilion or summerhouse, a place where there was music and dancing; nowhere was there any gambling! At night it was illuminated by myriads of white lights.

The Pleasure Beach remained open throughout the First World War – a place of relief from the horrors of fighting and death. After the war its popularity increased, and whilst the company became very successful, Alderman Bean remained a man of modest taste. He had financial interests in other pleasure parks at Morecambe and at Southport. Other new attractions were now developed including Noah's Ark, the Virginia Reel and in 1923 the

A tinted photo of 1906 – note how close high tide came to the stalls and machines and Maxim's Flying Machine – still in operation today

Big Dipper, using new undertrack friction wheels which allowed the designers to create steeper runs and more severe bends.

1925 was the year of the first Blackpool Illuminations and William Bean ensured that the Pleasure Beach played a full part in lighting up the town.

As chairman of the town's Finance Committee he steered the Borough forward to ever increasing success, as well as ensuring the continued growth of his own business. Sadly ill health prevented him from accepting the privilege of becoming mayor, and he died in January 1929 on a cruise and was buried at sea off the Canary Isles. Ernest Lawson, who had been one of his most critical opponents, wrote of him in the Blackpool Gazette:

'He desired more than anything else to devote his energies to making Blackpool the most modern, up-to-date and attractive seaside resort in the world.'

At the time of his death, William's only daughter, Doris, was living in London. She had recently married Leonard

The first major display of illuminations, 1925

Thompson, who had a degree in Natural Sciences from Oxford and post-graduate diplomas from universities in America and Sweden. With little heart-searching they decided to move north and inject youth and enthusiasm into the Pleasure Beach. They bought out the other partners and were soon making their presence felt at the Annual Conference of the National Association of Amusement Parks in New York.

In the 1930s several of the famous rides were reconstructed as the Corporation redrew the boundaries of the Pleasure Beach to fit in with road enhancement schemes. New attractions created during this decade included Blackpool's first Ferris Wheel – a No.16 Eli Wheel; the Ice Drome which replaced the roller skating rink and which seated 2,000 people; and the replacement Casino with its banqueting hall which seats 900 people – it later became known as the Wonderful World. By now the Pleasure Beach was recognised as the largest and most exciting amusement park in Britain, if not in Europe, and as a result Leonard Thompson was invited to organise the amusement park which accompanied the 1935 International Exposition which was held in Brussels. Whilst in Paris, working on the Exposition in 1937, he came across the Laughing Man in a Christmas display at the Galeries Lafayette. The accompanying Bing's Laughing Record drew the shoppers and after the sales

Fun has always been the watchword of the Pleasure Beach seen in this 1926 postcard and at the first birthday party of the Pepsi Max Big One, left

Leonard purchased it for the Pleasure Beach where it attracted great crowds. Unfortunately when the Fun House was destroyed in a fire in 1991 it was seriously damaged but has now been faithfully restored.

In 1938 Leonard purchased 11 acres of land at Morecambe creating there a pleasure park which is today known as Frontierland. The company has also held rights in the pleasure park at Southport, which was originally owned by the Corporation but which is now leased.

A serious fire in 1939 destroyed the Indian Theatre and much of the seating for the Ice Drome. The attractions stayed open but it was difficult to keep rides going except by cannibalising others.

After the war, in 1960, Leonard Thompson installed a Cableway, reminiscent of those in winter sports areas; it gave visitors a new perspective, both of the Pleasure Beach and Blackpool, but it was only the start of a major investment. Britain's first monorail was followed by the world's longest Log Flume.

The building of the M6 motorway, and the Blackpool spur (M55), made Blackpool even more attractive to visitors, and the future of the Pleasure Beach looked even brighter. Once again rides were brought from Expositions in distant parts of the world, such as the Monster brought from Montreal's Expo '67. In 1976 a vintage car museum was opened and the following year, again building on the love of nostalgia, an antique Carousel was installed.

Leonard Thompson died in 1976, but his son Geoffrey was ready to take on the mantle; already a director of the company – he became Managing Director, whilst his mother took on the role of company Chairman.

Already she had played an active role in the life of Blackpool, but now she applied her energies also to the Pleasure Beach. One of the first rides introduced by Geoffrey was the Steeplechase, in 1977, where on three parallel tracks twenty-four riders experience the thrill of the chase. The first looping coaster, the Revolution, came in 1979 followed by the Space Invader, and the Avalanche – an imitation bobsleigh ride where the trains of bobsleigh cars run freely down a curving channel.

By 1993 catering facilities were bringing in 25 per cent of the annual revenue, and live shows also started to proliferate – today the Paradise Room provides a modern theatre restaurant where an audience of 500 can sit down to dinner and then watch a spectacular stage show.

Succession has always been a real benefit in Blackpool Pleasure Beach and in 1994 Geoffrey and Barbara Thompson's daughter, Amanda, produced her first Hot Ice Show at Blackpool sharing the choreography with Robin Cousins. She has also been joined by brother Nicholas who has special responsibilities for catering, and sister Fiona, an architect, who uses her skills in the continual upgrading of the various areas in the complex.

Now... hold on to your stomach – here it comes; Geoffrey commissioned a ride which would take two years to build – the Pepsi Max Big One is the tallest and fastest roller-coaster in the world reaching a height of 235 feet before descending at speeds of up to 85mph, and a G force of 3.5. It cost nearly £13 million and its spectacular and graceful structure dominates Blackpool's promenade.

William Bean's dream is still alive, as vital to Blackpool Pleasure Beach's success as it has ever been.

IF YOU WANT A GOOD SHAKING, COME AND GO ON THE WHIP ON THE PLEASURE BEACH AT BLACKPOOL!

BLACKWOOD'S
BLACKPOOL ROCK

Blackpool Rock

Ingredients: Sugar, Glucose
Syrup,Flavouring and Colours
E102, E110, E122, E124,
E142, E129, E133.
R.D. BLACKWOOD (Prod.) Ltd.
BLACKPOOL FY4 4NE.

RDB with his wife Dorothy, Robert David Jnr, left, and Geoffrey.

Many will remember George Formby's famous song 'With my little stick of Blackpool Rock' – how much his audiences loved that song, and loved their Blackpool Rock.

It is widely thought that the first batch of Blackpool Rock was made in 1887 – in Dewsbury, by a man named Ben Bullock, who originally came from Burnley! He had made rock, with letters through it, for about twenty years, as well as other popular sweets at his Bullock's Excelsior Toffee Works in Dewsbury.

Whilst he was on holiday in Blackpool that year, staying at the Talbot Road Post Office, he realised the potential for sales of rock to the thousands of visitors who came to the resort each year. Whether he had the idea himself, or whether it was suggested to him by someone else, we do not know, but he was soon busy putting BLACKPOOL through his sticks of rock and sending them to the town to sell. It wasn't long before he was making similar rock for other seaside towns in various parts of the country, and other companies such as Brown's of Cleethorpes and John Bull at Bridlington were doing the same.

Blackpool Rock was first made in Blackpool in 1902. No one is sure who was the first manufacturer, but it may have been George Senior, an ex-Bullock's sugar boiler.

From as early as the beginning of the 18th century cottagers in Blackpool offered accommodation to visitors, but by 1780 hotels began to appear. In 1785 Lawrence Bailey advertised his 'commodious genteel house' in the hope that 'ladies and gentlemen may be pleased to favour him with their company'. The visitors, at that time, were the Lancashire gentry, merchants from Liverpool, manufacturers from Manchester and lawyers from Bolton. Advertisements in the Manchester press offered a coach setting off at 6am, stopping at the Black Bull at Preston for dinner, and arriving at 'Black pool' the same evening – this cost 14s.

In 1830 between 800 – 1,000 visitors came to the town. By 1851 this figure had risen to 2,000, and the resident population had also grown from a mere 473 in 1801 to over 7,000 by 1871. Blackpool's North Pier and Central Pier were both completed during the 1860s, and by 1870 a two mile section of the promenade had been built – which would all provide support to future sales of Blackpool Rock!

Towards the end of the last century Punch and Judy shows, buskers, acrobats and fortune tellers, donkey rides and vendors of patent medicines or rock jostled each other between the two wooden breakwaters opposite the New Inn and the Tower. Like market traders, the rock sellers used various pitchings, such as Billy Muggins who, wearing top hat and clogs, used to shout 'one for you, and one for you, and you...' as he threw bars of rock to people. Soon a crowd gathered, then he started selling the rock instead of giving it away. It was against the law to sell rock on the streets, but hawkers sold it from baskets both in the streets and on the beach, displaying the rock through the windows to guests eating their breakfasts in the boarding houses – it was regarded as part of the fun.

In the early years of the twentieth century a number of rock makers had started up in the town. One of these, The Exhibition Rock Company, had a stand at the 1924 Wembley Exhibition and sold Wembley Rock there. About this time companies well known to earlier generations were set up and included Waller & Hartley, Senior's, and the Coronation Rock Company.

During the 1930s Blackpool prospered, and so did the rock sellers. On a typical Saturday during the local mill town 'Wakes Weeks' and the period of the illuminations, over 300 trains would arrive, each

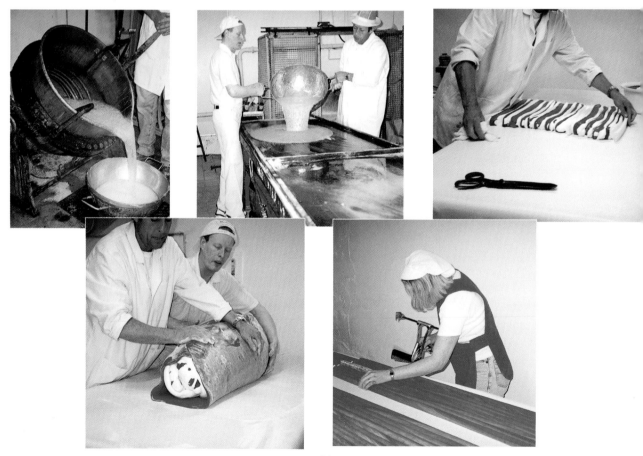

one packed with holidaymakers, each one, hopefully, taking home at least one stick of rock, probably more.

The Second World War brought a different influx of guests – servicemen in the Royal Air Force. 1940 saw the introduction of sugar rationing and with it the price of sugar almost doubled – rock makers became frustrated as demand exceeded supplies and visitors queued for sticks of rock.

One man, who came out of the Navy with an £80 gratuity and started selling rock, was Albert Gubay; later he developed the Kwik Save chain of stores and is now one of Britain's richest people. Another man who came to Blackpool about this time was Robert (Bob) David Blackwood. His father was a sweet wholesaler and Bob was born in Edinburgh, but he travelled many miles before he 'landed' in Blackpool. As a teenager Bob longed to travel to distant places as he looked at the ships in Leith Docks in Edinburgh. One day he discovered that a German cargo ship needed a cabin boy for a journey to Australia. He pleaded to go and feeling that, if the lad had a wanderlust he might as well

The finished product after boiling up the sugar and glucose, pouring out the hot toffee, forming the letters, assembling the batch and rolling it out into sticks.

get it out of his system while he was young, his father allowed him to go. Later he also went to South Africa and Canada.

On his return Bob worked as a salesman for a labelling company before starting to sell essences used by confectionery firms. It was this that brought him to Blackpool in 1944. One of the rock factories he visited, hoping to make a sale, was owned by Mr Addy. However, Mr Addy told him he did not want any essences as he was selling the business. Bob immediately asked him two questions – 'How much do you want for it?' and 'what is your sugar allocation?' The latter was an important question for at that time it decided the amount of rock he would be able to manufacture. Bob must have been satisfied with both answers for he bought the company.

The business also included a stall in Abingdon Street Market and a shop, and he soon acquired another shop, 13 Coronation Street, just opposite the Winter Gardens. It was an old fashioned sweet shop but it was a little gold mine. Soon the factory was working to capacity and the shop sold all he could produce, often exchanging sweets for sugar so he could make more!

In 1952 Bob went to meet Leonard Thompson, the owner of the Pleasure Beach, and they agreed that Blackwood's should have a stall on the main avenue where they could demonstrate making rock, humbugs and 'bananas', and of course sell

what they made – it was there for thirty years.

Today production is centred at the factory in Cowley Road. Bob Blackwood, a man of invention, created the cat-faced lollipops, Beatle Lollies, and also made Easter eggs, being the first to pipe on names.

Rock is mainly made from sugar, to which is added liquid glucose or corn syrup (the glucose prevents the sugar from crystallizing) and water. Most of the water boils away during the first part of the process as would the flavouring, so this is added later. The traditional pink mint rock is the most popular, and oil of peppermint is used to give its flavour and also that of humbugs, whereas aniseed is used in the distinctive flavoured brown rock. The intensity of colour is also important, for rock must be attractive to the eye as well as to the palate.

The sugar, glucose and water are heated together to a very high temperature in steam jacketed copper pans. The experienced sugar-boiler carefully controls the temperature and after about 15 minutes the hot liquid is tipped onto water cooled tables where it quickly cools. The batch is divided into two parts, one to be kept clear. To the other is added colouring, pink for the portion

CONVICT ROCK

PORT ARTHUR TASMANIA
LETTERED ROCK CANDY
Net 50g
Ingredients: Sugar, Glucose Syrup, Artificial Colours 102, 133, 129, 122, 142.
Made in England by
R. D. Blackwood Ltd. Blackpool
for Blackpool Rock Dist. P.O. Box 306 Albury

which is to form the coating and red to that which is used in the lettering. The uncoloured portion is then transferred to a 'pulling machine' which aerates it, the presence of air making the rock become white. The flavouring, only a few teaspoonfuls, is now added. The red coloured batch is placed on a heated table to prevent it becoming brittle and the letters are formed. The rock is then assembled and finally its pink coating is added. After it has been formed into a conical shape 4 feet long, about 12 inches wide at its widest and 6 inches wide at the other end, it is rolled and stretched until it reaches the required size. Now it can be cut into lengths and wrapped.

In 1952 Bob married, not only acquiring a wife, Dorothy, but also a stepson, Geoffrey, who is now managing director of the company, and has himself worked in rock making for over forty years. By the age of fourteen Geoffrey was sitting in the shop window demonstrating the art of chocolate-dipping! Their son Robert David Blackwood Jnr is now also a director of the company.

Geoffrey and his wife Margaret, who wrote The Story of Blackpool Rock, are both involved with Blackwood's and have seen it develop into a wholesale company that exports rock to Australia!

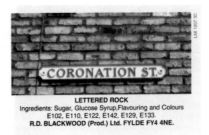

LETTERED ROCK
Ingredients: Sugar, Glucose Syrup, Flavouring and Colours
E102, E110, E122, E142, E129, E133.
R.D. BLACKWOOD (Prod.) Ltd. FYLDE FY4 4NE.

BODDINGTONS BREWERY

There is evidence, in a street directory, that Strangeways brewery existed in 1794, but it is believed it was actually founded in 1778. In 1794 it was operated by Caistor and Fray who were brewers and corn dealers. The brewery stood to the north of the River Irk, which at that time marked the northern boundary of Manchester. Over succeeding years the business partners changed and in 1828 it traded as Hole, Potter and Harrison, ale and porter brewers. Samuel Hole's son later became Dean Hole of Rochester, famous as a long time President of the National Rose Society.

For many generations the Boddington family had been corn millers in Oxfordshire and Buckinghamshire. Brothers John, born 1807, and Henry, born 1813, decided to move north when the family fell upon hard times. John went to work as a mill foreman in Stockport, but then moved to work for Hole, Potter and Harrison in the accounts department in 1831; Henry joined his brother in 1832 working for the brewery as a traveller.

John Boddington left the brewery in about 1835 and set up as a corn and provisions agency at Ashton-under-Lyne. Henry however continued to work at the Strangeways Brewery and in 1853 became sole proprietor. After 75 years of trading the brewery took on another new name, Henry Boddington, still familiar today, although the firm is now part of the Whitbread group.

At that time Strangeways was on the edge of the built up area and housed Strangeways Hall and Strangeways House, with their grounds and gardens, as well as the Assize Courts, but at that time no prison. Access to the west had been provided by the iron Waterloo Bridge over the River Irwell, an important link, for a few years later the brewery was offering a free delivery service to families living within six miles of the city.

The earliest known advertisement for the company is in the Manchester Directory of 1854-55 offering 'Pale Ale Brewed Especially for Private Families'. By 1863, using an impressive Royal Coat of Arms, they were offering 'Light Dinner Beer 1s a gallon'.

In 1859 Henry took a John Hart into partnership, trading as Henry Boddington & Co, but the partnership was dissolved in 1871. With some difficulty Henry bought out Hart's one third share and again became sole proprietor. In 1870 Henry's son, also Henry, joined the business, to be followed in 1879 by his brother, Robert Slater Boddington.

It was Henry Jnr who put into working order the Bridge Brewery at Burton-on-Trent, aptly named as it is built on an island spanned by the Trent bridge. His father bought the brewery to

The counting house, 1906

meet the growing preference of the public for pale beers, rather than porter, taking the view that only the water at Burton would make really fine pale beers.

Back at Strangeways, in 1877, Boddingtons constructed new premises in Mary Street, on the banks of the River Irwell. They used the premises as stables, trading also as 'a cow-keeper, dairyman or purveyor of milk', and later also having a cooperage there. They had a town office from about 1870 at 6 Victoria Street, Royal Exchange, but in 1877 new general offices were built at the brewery and a telephone linked the two.

With Henry Boddington as proprietor output grew steadily until in 1872 50,000 barrels a year were produced; by 1877 this figure had more than doubled and they were now the largest brewers in Manchester. In 1878 they employed 238 staff, spread between the two breweries and the branch stores at Birmingham, Rochdale and Crewe, and owned a total of 71 public houses and beer houses and had another 32 pubs on occupation leases.

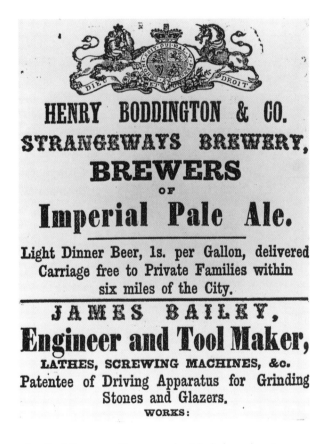

HENRY BODDINGTON & CO. STRANGEWAYS BREWERY, BREWERS OF Imperial Pale Ale.

Light Dinner Beer, 1s. per Gallon, delivered Carriage free to Private Families within six miles of the City.

JAMES BAILEY, Engineer and Tool Maker, LATHES, SCREWING MACHINES, &c. Patentee of Driving Apparatus for Grinding Stones and Glazers. WORKS:

In 1881 the great brewery chimney – which still dominates the Strangeways skyline – was built and during the decade new boiling pans, slate tanks and cask hoists were installed. In 1883 Henry Boddington Snr retired, and died three years later. Following his retirement the company became a limited company, Henry Boddington & Co Ltd, with three of Henry's four sons as directors – Henry, William and Robert. In 1887 it became a public company, Boddingtons' Breweries Ltd. In 1888 Sandywell Brewery at Greengate in Salford was acquired, along with 17 pubs, from George Robert Clayton, who then became a director of Boddingtons.

In view of later developments, Boddington's visit in 1888 to see Robert Baker of Whitbread & Co was interesting. In 1869 he had been appointed by Whitbread as their agent to begin bottling beer, a business that had grown significantly, but the Boddington directors decided that the time was not yet right for them to do so. However, we know that bottling was commenced by 1890.

Boddingtons now felt it appropriate to close the brewery at Burton; at first it was leased to Leicester brewers Everard, Son & Welldon but was finally sold in 1899.

Meanwhile Henry Boddington Jnr had retired in 1891, a rich man who was an influential figure in Manchester. He was an original director and enthusiastic supporter of the Manchester Ship Canal Company, a local councillor, trustee of many charities and sidesman at Manchester Cathedral.

He was only 42 when he retired and continued to lead an active life on the Pownall Hall estate at Wilmslow until his death in 1925.

William Slater Boddington became the next chairman, a post he held until his death in 1908, aged 55. During the period of his chairmanship the company bought some significant properties from J Chetham of Heaton Norris and purchased William Sumner's brewery at Fulwood, Preston. Among the Sumner outlets was the Sumners Hotel at Fulwood Barracks, said to be 'one of the most valuable licensed premises in the district'. The company's position in the Preston area was further strengthened when in 1899 they purchased Hull's brewery in Glover Street, which they then closed. In 1903 they acquired part of the share capital of the Isle of Man Breweries (1903) Ltd and the following year it became Boddingtons (IOM) Ltd. This was disposed of in 1922. After two explosions of malt dust at Strangeways in 1891, extra precautions were introduced and in 1902 the old portion of the brewery was remodelled.

In 1893 Boddingtons were supplying in cask Pale Ale(A), Mild Ale(BB), Strong Ale(CC), Bitter Beer(IP), Stout(S), and Extra Stout(SS), and in bottles Pale Ale, Bitter Beer and Stout as well as a range of wines and spirits. By 1896 Pale Ale was available in Champagne Quarts, and Family Stout and Strangeways Stout had been added to the bottled beer range.

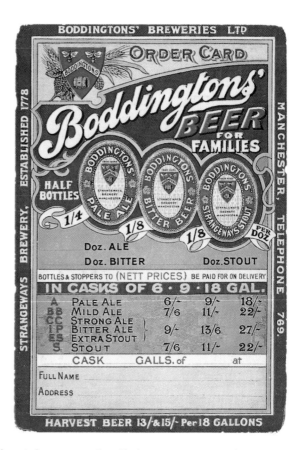

During Robert Boddington's period of chairmanship there was consolidation and many improvements were made to the brewery. In the 1920s a new bottling hall was constructed and slate vessels were replaced with aluminium ones.

In 1911 striking railway workers, supported by dockers, prevented delivery of malt and sugar from Manchester stations and supplies had to be carted from suburban stations to Strangeways; similarly beer had to go by lorry to several destinations.

Trade was badly hit by the great depression in the 1920s and 1930s and the profits of the brewery fell by more than half. In 1924 there was the suggestion that a motorway might be built between Coventry and Manchester and that for a contribution of £5,000 Boddingtons could have the right to supply all the canteens on the route – many years were to pass before such a motorway became reality! When Robert Slater Boddington died in 1930 he was the final link with the original board of 1887. He had worked at the brewery for 51 years, including 42 years as managing director and 22 years as chairman. For 25 years he was chairman of the Manchester Brewers' Association, and at the time of his death was vice-chairman of the Brewers' Society. He was succeeded by his sons, Philip as chairman and joint managing director, and Geoffrey as joint managing director.

During the Second World War the brewery was badly damaged in the worst air raid Manchester had experienced, on 22 December 1940. Production at the brewery came to a standstill and could not restart for seven months, but the destruction gave an opportunity for reconstruction after the war.

The brewery was also expanded onto adjoining land, but still the company was at risk from takeover bids. To strengthen its position Boddingtons entered into a trading agreement with Whitbread and Ind Coope Tetley Ansell in 1962, which meant that products of both groups could be sold in Boddingtons 600 houses and Boddingtons would brew draught beer for Whitbread. The position was further strengthened in 1962 when they acquired the Reddish brewery at Stockport and its 67 associated houses. These wise decisions enabled them to resist the bid from Allied Breweries in 1969.

During the 1970s further modernisation of the plant took place at Strangeways, and new labels were introduced for bottled beers and wines and spirits featuring a new logo with new house colours. It still incorporated the traditional barrel and bees, the latter symbolising a hive of industry, as on Manchester's coat of arms. In 1975 Boddingtons began brewing Whitbread Forest Brown and were soon producing 12,000 barrels a year.

In 1982 Oldham Brewery was acquired for £24.5 million and three years later Higson's Brewery in Liverpool was bought at a cost of £27.5 million. Ewart Boddington retired in 1989 and for the first time since 1853 the company was not run by a Boddington. That same year Whitbread acquired the brewing interests of Boddingtons for £50.7 million, including Higson's brewery and the related brands. Now, as part of a major national brewery, they were able to have muscle and the full range of outlets. Following major investment at Strangeways, the brewery can now produce 600,000 barrels a year, but this is expected to rise to over a million barrels in the near future. However, the Boddington Pub Group retained the Boddington pubs, the drinks retailing division of the Boddington Group plc.

All beers brewed at Strangeways are made with water drawn from 200 feet beneath the brewery and traditional raw materials such as English Pale Ale Malt and whole leaf aroma hops, including famous old English varieties 'Fuggles' and 'Goldings'. The strain of yeast, with which the beers are fermented, is also unique to Boddingtons. Strangeways is the only brewery in the world producing the beer with the thick white head, 'Cream of Manchester', a name now known across the whole of Britain. Latest technology has enabled home drinkers to savour beers with this same creamy head as the brewery has introduced the 'draughtflow can' which is fitted with a little 'widget'.

Boddingtons beers are now becoming known in many other parts of the world as export markets are developed in Europe, Japan, South Africa, Canada, USA, and Australasia.

BODDINGTONS. THE CREAM OF MANCHESTER.
Courtesy of the ingenious new Draughtflow system, you can now enjoy the smooth flavour and creamy head of handpulled Boddingtons from a can. Brewed at the Strangeways Brewery since 1778.

BOOTHS
supermarkets

1912.
Xmas Fruit Report.

In 1897 the founder of the company wrote down the story of his life. He described how his early years began in times of great hardship and sorrow, and continued through years of difficulty and insecurity. He had to face problems which were ultimately overcome by persistent industry, wise use of what little money he had, and a firm faith in the overruling power of Providence. He saw the purpose of his autobiography as being to encourage other poor orphan boys or struggling youths to progress in life.

Edwin Henry Booth was born in Bury about 1828. His mother was one of the younger daughters of a family of twelve children, and married when she was 18. She had a son and a daughter by her first husband, but he died when they were young. She then moved to Bury where she met and married a Dr Booth, who had a large practice in the town, and Edwin was born soon afterwards. Her new-found happiness was short lived for her second husband also died, from an accident, and they were left unprovided for and in poverty. Later his mother married once more, but this was a most unhappy relationship in which Edwin suffered greatly. The stepfather was often violent when he was drunk and often swore that he would kill the young lad if he found him on his premises.

When Edwin was only ten he was left to fend for himself, unwanted by his stepfather, his mother afraid for his safety if he stayed in the house. Once he walked the fourteen miles to Manchester to find a friend, and on other occasions a similar distance to Bolton. In Bolton, when he was eleven, he managed to get a job as an errand boy, but often didn't finish his work until near midnight. He earned three shillings a week and gave one shilling to an old lady in whose house he boarded; this left him

with only two shillings to clothe and feed himself. For breakfast he had only thin porridge and a piece of dry bread; for dinner a herring with a piece of bread or a potato. For a change he would have a 1d basin of soup, taking with him a piece of bread in his pocket.

Sir Edwin Booth

At teatime it was warm water with a pinch of tea and a little milk and sugar and a slice of bread. And supper, only rarely, when he was invited out by some friend. Things went on like this for twelve months, but still he trusted in God, and longed for someone who might take an interest in him.

Eventually when he asked for a holiday he walked twenty-one miles to see his half-sister, but when he arrived back a day late he was sacked. After this he got a job in a draper's shop, and then one in a grocer's where he lived in the grocer's house, but was paid no wage! Eventually he moved to Preston.

To advance himself he got up at five every morning and studied until eight before he started the day's work; at the end of the day he studied until eleven o'clock or midnight. He was paid £18 a year. After his stepfather's death he also used some of this money to help his mother.

By now Edwin was about 19. Blackpool was becoming a 'rising watering place' and with the help of a Mr Nickson he rented a barn, which had been converted into a shop. He employed a lad at 5s a week and worked night and day to get the grocery business started and placed on a successful footing. Never had he been so happy.

The next year he persuaded his landlord to pull down the barn and build a fine new shop on the site and from there he attracted trade from many hotels and schools in the town and quickly saw considerable profits.

He married Susannah Phillips, the daughter of a Colne corn-miller, and they set up home in a house he had built in Blackpool. Eventually they expanded the business, opening a shop in Chorley, and moved to the town to live. They had a son and a daughter, but sadly lost their little girl when she was only four years old. After they moved to Preston they had a further three sons and three daughters, although one of these died from diptheria.

From the early years in Preston Edwin showed a great concern for the poor and destitute orphans of the town. At that time it was normal for them to be sent to the workhouse, but with the help of friends Edwin formed a society to help such children, ensuring that they went to day and Sunday schools, were fostered and clothed. Eventually money was provided to buy an old estate, enabling him to build an orphanage with accommodation for 120 children. The site also had park-like grounds and its own little church.

During this time the business had continued to grow and Edwin's four sons all joined it. However, two of them left, one to become a doctor, the other to enter the wholesale tea trade in London. The eldest son, John Booth, became a junior partner in 1881, and gradually took more and more responsibility. The business became a private limited company in 1896, with headquarters at Preston and shops at Blackpool, Chorley, Lytham and Blackburn.

Edwin Booth died in 1899 – he had created a good business from very difficult beginnings; he had been a fine Christian gentleman who had served his local community well. John Booth now became chairman and the youngest son, Tim, became a director, along with William Tattersall, a long serving employee of the firm.

John had been a delicate boy and to improve his health his parents sent him on a voyage to the Mediterranean where he visited Greece and Turkey. As a result he took a great interest in cargoes of sultanas and currants.

SUPPLEMENT TO SHOP EQUIPMENT & SHOPFITTING NEWS, MAY 1964

● *Transformation at Booths of Preston. See page 7*

Self-Service Review
AND GUIDE TO THE SHOP EQUIPMENT EXHIBITION

This supplement to Shop Equipment & Shopfitting News sets out the wide range of equipment available today for the self-service retailer and those contemplating making the change to self-service — not only the grocer, but also the hardware store, chemist, departmental and chain store etc. This information will also be of value, either for immediate or future reference, to architects, shopfitters, designers and every progressive retailer whatever his trade. To speed you full information on any product mentioned in this review complete the Reader Enquiry Form at the back of this issue and send to the address on the reverse side.

Booths pioneering self-service hits the headlines in this 1964 Shop Equipment News supplement and, overleaf, more style setting at Booths in Carnforth

He had admired the profit sharing scheme operated by Lever Brothers at Port Sunlight and in 1909 he introduced a similar scheme to Booths – he called it their 'bonus scheme', and it applied to everyone, even down to the errand boy. He also continued his father's work with the Harris Orphanage and worked for the Home and Workshops for the Blind. He died at his home in Bowness in 1941, aged 85. His two elder sons, E H (Wyn) Booth and J K (Kenny) Booth, entered the business in 1906 and 1910 respectively. Their father gave them early opportunities to gain management experience and in due time they became directors.

After the First World War the company expanded rapidly with the opening of shops in Ashton, Leyland, St Anne's on Sea, Longton, and a further shop in Blackpool, on the South Shore. In the 1930s premises were opened on Lord Street in Southport and also in Kendal, Broughton, and at Penwortham. About this time the board of directors was also enlarged to include three further members of staff, Tom Wiggans, H W Tomlinson, and A Hampson.

In 1947 Booths celebrated their centenary. Wyn Booth died in 1951 and was succeeded as chairman by Kenny Booth. In 1954 sales reached £1 million, a notable achievement for the time. Profits steadily rose until 1960, when the first supermarket appeared. Up to that time a third of Booths business was delivery on credit and they felt they could not cut prices. In the autumn of 1961 the decision was made that they must change their approach and the shops at Fulwood and Leyland were converted to self service stores. Improved sales were immediate and within a few weeks they could see their way forward. In 1962 the shops were making a three and a half per cent increase, but the two self service stores a twenty per cent increase; it was obvious the others must also be converted.

All the new business was on a cash basis, and in order to phase out the order trade an increasing charge was made for delivery, although the company took every reasonable step it could not to upset long standing customers. Due to the increase in cash sales, by 1966 total sales had reached £2 million a year. Year by year further shops were modernised to meet the new trading patterns.

In 1970 Kenny Booth died, aged 78, having completed sixty years with the company. John Booth became chairman and Eric Woodhouse was made a director. It was not until 1973 that it was possible to open up new sites; the first was at Torrisholme near Morecambe, followed by Garstang, Lancaster, Clitheroe, and Windermere. That year Edwin J Booth joined the firm, a fifth generation member of the family business. Other family members, Simon Booth and Graham Booth, joined the business whilst Edwin Booth and company secretary Neil Standing became directors.

In 1982 sales reached over £27 million and for the first time profits exceeded £1 million. 1986 saw the opening of a new store at Marton, Blackpool, although other town centre stores, which had no car parking facilities, were closed down about this time as part of the firms re-evaluation of trading policy.

Expansion into new areas has been carefully planned, the first of these ventures being to Knutsford in Cheshire, where a store was opened in 1990, and this has been followed by stores in Ulverston, and Ilkley in Yorkshire.

BROADBENTS & BOOTHROYDS

William Ashton, writing in the Southport Journal in 1922, recalled John Broadbent's shop at 54 Tulketh Street as an 'all sorts shop'; in Green's Directory for 1868 it sold groceries, provisions, beer, bread, flour and confectionery, tea and smallwares. Sometime before 1876 John moved his business to 19 Chapel Street, and also traded at Market Passage (now Corporation Street), where he concentrated on small-wares and hosiery – he was now a wholesaler as well as retailer.

By 1880 Broadbent had expanded into 21 Chapel Street, and also had premis-

LORD STREET AND CAMBRIDGE HALL.

es at 13 Cambridge Arcade, which was his 'Bon Marché', no doubt imitating the now famous Parisian store. His sales interests included patent medicines, drapery, hosiery, gloves, smallwares and trimmings – in his advertisements he calls the 'special attention of the Ladies of Southport and Birkdale to the NEW DEPARTMENTS recently added to his Establishment', trying to attract both middle and lower income groups as customers. Year by year new lines were added; by 1882 these included tailoring, dressmaking and stationery, and a few years later he opened a wholesale and brush warehouse at 17 Victoria Market. Before the end of the decade he adopted the name 'Bon Marché' for his entire premises in Chapel Street and Cambridge Arcade, at which stage he was proud to exclaim 'Broadbents sell everything'.

However, the expansion of the business put a severe strain on John Broadbent and in 1887 he sold

it to Conway Stidston, a native of Plymouth, who took the name Broadbent, becoming Conway Stidston Broadbent. He also rapidly expanded the firm and by 1894 it comprised 11,13,15,17 Cambridge Arcade and 17,19,21 Chapel Street. Before the turn of the century 'Lifeboat Serge' was a great seller at 6½ d per yard; a full dress length in navy blue, black, cream or cardinal cost between 10s 6d and 17s 6d.

Stidston Broadbent entered into the political and commercial life of Southport; he joined the committee of the Temperance Society, became involved with the mission at Parbold and was appointed secretary of the Unionist Association – in 1894 he became a councillor and sat on the Parks and Cemetery, Health, Highways and School Attendance committees.

In 1896 the business became a limited company with the title 'Broadbents Bon Marché Limited'; Stidston became its chairman and managing director. So expansion could take place, the company issued 2,000 preference shares at £5 each – the offer was oversubscribed by 1,630 shares, so high was Broadbents' reputation, and the company gave priority of share allocation to people in Southport and Birkdale to strengthen customer loyalty.

When the secretary's position became vacant in 1897, Arthur Edwin Mercy persuaded Stidston to give him the job. Arthur had been orphaned when he was two and was brought up in a Birmingham orphanage until he was thirteen, when he went to work as a clerk at a Birmingham drapery business.

The firm hit difficult times when Stidston Broadbent involved it in a disastrous purchase of Stoke Newington Bon Marché shares. However, accommodation was leased in premises which adjoined the store and trade was expanded over

THE BON MARCHÉ

three floors. These negotiations were carried out by Arthur Mercy and in 1903 he was given a seat on the Board. After the Stoke Newington affair Stidston Broadbent appears to have lost his enthusiasm and eventually he and his son Edgar sold a lot of their shares to Arthur who in 1908 became sole general manager; in 1914 he became managing director.

He had recently renegotiated the leases of much of the property, giving them 20 year terms, and now decided to alter and enhance the buildings.

At this time girls were usually taken on a two year apprenticeship. They lived in a hostel that Broadbents provided and were given their board and keep, but parents had to make arrangements for their washing, provide a black dress and give the girls pocket money. By 1913 conditions improved – in their first year they received 1s a week pocket money from the firm, in their second year 2s 6d! Senior assistants, who had regular contact with customers, were carefully recruited by Arthur Mercy, often being selected from other areas of the country; similar care was taken in appointing buyers.

After the difficult years of the First World War, Arthur Mercy set about purchasing the premises they occupied. New departments, including a funeral service, were introduced, and the store continued to prosper.

Broadbents was a remarkable story – in 1910 turnover was just over £33,000; by 1921 it had risen to £135,000, but even in the difficult years it never fell below £147,000. As early as 1930 Arthur Mercy started to consider schemes for hire purchase and other sales initiatives, such as 'National Cotton Week', which offered bargains on Lancashire products.

Although the Second World War brought its

Left: advert for Broadbents, 1886 and, right, the store in the early twenties.

problems Arthur realised that at the end of it there would be people who would have 'money to burn'.

After the war, modernisation of the store began once again and its management was strengthened by the appointment to the Board of Arthur's two sons-in-law. Vyvian V Pedlar, who had his own retail business in Southport's Wayfarers Arcade, was appointed in 1947 and Reuben Hainsworth, a woollen manufacturer of Farsley in Yorkshire, in 1949. Geoffrey Foster, an accountant, was appointed a director in 1948, and became joint managing director with Arthur Mercy in 1951 when Arthur Mercy was 77! Arthur Mercy finally relinquished the managing directorship two years later, although he remained as titular chairman until his death in 1959.

When Vyvian Pedlar became chairman he sought a firm control of the company to protect its independence from national store chains. Arthur Mercy's shares had been inherited by Kathleen Hainsworth and Margaret Pedlar, but the Hainsworths were more concerned with their woollen interests. Shares were exchanged for cash to increase the Pedlars' holding of the company, and in 1963 the family attained a voting majority. In 1962 Anthony Pedlar, younger son of Vyvian, was appointed a director having gained experience in other companies, and he became managing director in 1964.

By the 1970s Broadbents had grown to occupy the whole of the site from Cambridge Arcade to

Corporation Street, and as far back towards Lord Street as the Corporation offices – it had a unified facade, one of the most impressive in Southport.

★ ★ ★

William Jolley began as a linen and woollen draper in Southport in 1823, in a house in Richmond Hill, where the Atkinson Library now stands. Most of the stock consisting of handkerchiefs, womens 'caps', lace and haberdashery and material with which women could make their underwear would be kept in drawers or boxes, wrapped in paper packets.

In 1833 he transferred to Lord Street and the following year took on Samuel Boothroyd as an assistant. Samuel was born in Pontefract in 1814, one of the children of the Rev Dr Boothroyd, a Congregational minister. Rev George Greatbatch, a friend of Dr Boothroyd, believed that the Southport air would be good for Samuel's health and it was a natural step for him to join Jolley, who was also a Congregationalist. In 1835 they became partners in the business, William contributing £700 and Samuel £400; both men also later married daughters of Rev. Greatbatch.

The partners transferred their business to London & Manchester House on Lord Street in 1844 – it boasted lofty plate glass windows, a dome, gallery and pillars, complete with terracotta capitals and bases. The internal fittings were worthy of a drawing room, and the partners were now described as silk mercers and general drapers. Edward Johnson

BOOTHROYDS,
295 to 309,
Lord Street, Southport.

SILK MERCERS, DRAPERS, COSTUMIERS, MILLINERS, LADIES' & CHILDREN'S OUTFITTERS.

FUNERAL FURNISHERS

MILLINERY SHOWROOM.

● ● ●   *Telephone* **1045**—*Two Lines.*

Established **1830.**

Telegrams: BOOTHROYDS, Southport.

Rimmer was raised on a farm in Birkdale, and rather than train to be a druggist in Liverpool, where it was feared he might fall into sinful ways, he was apprenticed to Jolley & Boothroyd in 1845; William was also his Sunday School teacher.

William stood as a candidate for the town's Improvement Commissioners in 1851, but died a few days before the election took place, aged 51. Sarah Jolley, William's widow, now became a partner, remaining so until her retirement in 1860. The following year Benjamin, Samuel's eldest son, and E J Rimmer joined the partnership and the business traded as 'Boothroyd, Son & Company'. Samuel had now become involved in the Association for the Improvement and Prosperity of Southport, and worked for the development of a pier – in 1860 a 1,200 yard long pier was opened.

About this time Samuel took as an apprentice Benjamin Waugh, who was born in Settle in 1839, but who left the business in 1862 to train as a Congregational minister. He later married Samuel's daughter, Sarah. During his ministry at Greenwich he worked with neglected and ill-treated children and later was involved in the forming of the London Society for the Prevention of Cruelty to Children. In 1895, by Royal Charter, this became the National Society for the Prevention of Cruelty to Children, and Benjamin Waugh became its director until 1905.

Boothroyds expanded into other adjacent premises on Lord Street (a total frontage of 84 feet) and additions were made to the rear of the shop – they now added boots, shoes, and furniture to their merchandise. There was also a house for the apprentices and unmarried staff, workshops and a 'house for the hearse'.

Samuel made frequent business visits to Paris, London and Liverpool. In advertisements of 1868 the business was described as being drapers, silk merchants, cabinet makers, upholsterers, carpet warehousemen and Venetian blind makers. In 1875-6 sales climbed to a peak of £70,369; the business traded as Boothroyd Son & Rimmer's, and in 1881 they held their first show of summer fashions.

More sons joined the partnership as Samuel became more involved in local politics, standing as a Liberal – he had already been mayor in 1869-70, and was mayor again in 1878-79 and 1879-80. When he died in 1886 the Southport Guardian reported 'We don't know one whose contribution to the welfare of the town has been greater than his...'

Despite Samuel's death the partnership agreement continued to run until its expiry in 1893 when Benjamin also retired. He was presented with an illuminated address to mark his retirement, to which 154 employees had subscribed. In 1895 E J Rimmer celebrated fifty years with Boothroyds.

A new partnership was created in 1900 between Alfred Boothroyd, William Jolley Boothroyd, his son Philip Douglas Boothroyd and E J Rimmer. E J Rimmer died in 1907, shortly after his retirement – he had been a Liberal councillor and alderman, magistrate and mayor, and a fervent Congregationalist.

In 1914 Boothroyds stopped selling furniture and carpets, intending to use the space to expand drapery sales, but as this coincided with the outbreak of the First World War it could have seemed unpatriotic. Instead they encouraged customers to buy goods of British manufacture!

From 1917, with all the partners being members of the family, the firm's title was changed to 'Boothroyds'. 1925 saw the celebration of Boothroyds' centenary and special displays and sales took place, including linen specially woven for the British Empire Exhibition which had been held at Wembley the previous year – they claimed to be the only store in the north to have such articles for sale.

Boothroyds continued to be run by members of the Boothroyd family until 1971 when they decided to sell the business. Broadbents took the unusual step of buying another department store in the same town because Anthony Pedlar, the managing director of Broadbents held the view that the management team at Broadbents was strong enough to manage two stores.

In 1982, a much needed major refurbishment of the Boothroyds' store was undertaken. Unfortunately before this was completed, Anthony Pedlar died aged 49, and his widow, Mary, became chairman and managing director. During the 1980s the two stores continued to flourish and build on the investment which the founding families had made in Southport, but in 1990 the decision was made, for family reasons, to sell them. They were acquired by Owen Owen, a Liverpool based retail business with a strong family business tradition.

Unfortunately in 1993 Owen Owen were forced to put the two businesses on the market again. The Chapel Street Store (Broadbents) was acquired by BHS and the Lord Street Store by Beales, a family owned department store group based in Bournemouth. Today it continues to trade under the name of Broadbents and Boothroyds. The original Broadbents business still remains (now called Lord Street Properties) and retains the ownership of the freehold of the Lord Street store as well as the Wayfarers Arcade adjacent to it.

Brooke Bond

Arthur Brooke was born above the shop in George Street, Ashton-under-Lyne in 1845. As a four-year-old he used to enjoy clambering onto the large wheelbarrow, piled high with packets of tea, and have a ride through the terraced streets as his father's porter made his deliveries. Arthur's grandfather, an NCO in the Scots Guards, had been killed in the battle of Waterloo and young Arthur was educated by the Waterloo Fund which had been set up to provide for the dependent children of soldiers.

Arthur's father, Charles, built up a good business as a wholesale tea merchant and although initially the family lived over the warehouse, the ground floor of a terraced house in George Street, they later moved to a house out of town.

Tea had become popular as Indian estates provided more tea and as the developing railways in this country made distribution to the provincial towns quicker and cheaper. No longer was it a select drink just for the upper classes. However, with Arthur having had a good education, his father was keen that his son should enter the most fashionable trade of the day, and in Lancashire that was cotton!

During the American Civil War the mill in which Arthur had become a partner failed and at the age of nineteen he became a pupil in the Liverpool branch of a wholesale tea company. A hard working youth, he was soon transferred to the company's headquarters in London at £1 a week.

After hearing that the family business was declining he returned home and threw all his energies into it, often walking many miles to secure orders in isolated villages. During these long walks he thought about the future and when he had saved £400 he decided to start his own business. This idea received support from his friends, and in 1869 he opened the doors of 29 Market Street, Manchester – opposite the Royal Exchange – and put up the sign 'Brooke, Bond and Company'. There was no 'Mr Bond', the name just sounded good. Market Street was a bustling shopping street, thronged with housewives who were keen to buy the only items he sold, tea, coffee and sugar, and always 'cash only' sales – something unusual, but many businesses were crippled by credit and debt.

Arthur Brooke

Arthur Brooke developed premium blends of tea, taking care to choose exact proportions from a selected range of teas – taste, colour, leaf size, changing seasons and climatic conditions were, and are, important. His blends did not vary, they were true to their description and were weighed out into full weight ½lb and 1lb bags. His lowest price tea was 4d lb for rich new sappy tea, whereas his most expensive one, at 4s lb, was a particularly choice rich Indian Pekoe.

He wrote 'Brooke Bond & Co' in his own flowing script and used this as his trade mark; he created his own window cards advertising the products using terms which drew attention to their quality and reliability.... 'Deliciously Rich', Ripe, Juicy, Fragrant', 'the Creme de la Creme'. He was one of the first to use newspaper advertising in an amusing way.

His business flourished and by 1872, with shops in Liverpool, Leeds and Bradford, he felt it was now time for him to move to London, leaving the northern shops under the control of his Leeds manager. He took a warehouse in Whitechapel High Street, near Petticoat Lane, and opened two shops in the City, but they were not a success and were soon closed.

The same year that Arthur Brooke started his business his mother died and his father sold his business at Ashton, married again and moved to London.

Arthur's health also soon broke down, due to overwork, and he took a sea voyage to Egypt, leaving his father in charge of the firm.

On his return Arthur again took control of the company; by the age of thirty he was earning £5,000 a year. In 1875 he married and set up home in an elegant house in Stonebridge Park, Willesden, but even on their honeymoon business crept in when he took his new wife to visit a printer who specialised in producing coloured-showcards in a Paris back-street.

By the late 1870s a depression hit Britain, particularly in the industrial north. In Bradford he found previous customers begging for goods, and for the first time he relaxed his no credit rule; he also sold his Scottish shops and looked at ways of reducing his own standard of living. He sold his large house and moved to a smaller one, and he gave up his carriage, sending his coachman to look after the van horses in Leeds. If times were bad he made sure the head of the firm took the first cut!

About this time a grocer asked if he might buy Brooke Bond tea in bulk at wholesale rates and Arthur realised others might wish to do this. Now he started to circulate grocers advertising blended tea, but of course 'cash with order'. Soon the orders came in and by 1887 the company had turned the corner. Once again he could consider his own comforts, and he bought a house in Kensington and a country house at Dorking.

In 1892 the firm became 'Brooke Bond and Company Limited', with a share capital of £150,000 and a working capital of £5,000. The goodwill, trade-marks and beneficial interest in the various leases of the premises were valued at £100,000. The business was now primarily wholesale, but he kept the shops in the north, not least to keep the needs of the customer and the trade in perspective. Arthur Brooke became chairman and managing director.

The staff proudly boasted that orders received in the 8 o'clock post in the morning were despatched on the 9 o'clock trains! Increasing sales of packet tea led to the appointment of agents. On Queen Victoria's 80th birthday the

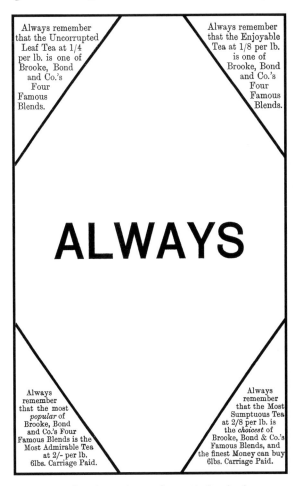

A very early advert (around 1883) for the famous tea

Brooke Bond shops gave 1lb of tea to every customer aged over 80. A few years later in 1902, they produced red-white-and-blue caddies which bore the portraits of King Edward VII and Queen Alexandra. Sales aids had to be more than gimmicks – Arthur Brooke would ask 'Ah, yes, but will it help sell a pound of tea?'

A branch was opened in Calcutta in 1901, both as a means of buying tea for Britain and also to start selling packeted tea in India, where it had been traditionally sold loose. The company also sold on an agency basis British biscuits, coffee, matches and tinned milk.

In 1907 the company started deliveries in the north using horse vans and got rid of the wholesale agents. The idea succeeded and was soon brought into effect in London. In 1909 they bought the patents for equipment for boiling water for tea and coffee making and set up a wholly-owned subsidiary, Jackson Boilers Ltd. The following year they signed a contract with the Admiralty for the supply of tea to the Navy and soon signed a further one with the War Office for the Army. When Arthur Brooke retired his son Gerald became chairman.

From 1911 the tea factories had started to become mechanised and motor vans were also introduced – the little red Trojan vans were to become a symbol of the company. Wartime brought its own pressures, not least when civil servants decided tea was 'an unnecessary import!' Quickly the company bought the San Paulo coffee business, but under public pressure the earlier edict was rescinded.

"IT'S HERE!"

The New Season's Tea has arrived! This appetising announcement excites a thrill of expectant pleasure in millions of minds. It's an annual event welcomed eagerly by English womankind especially. What longing for the fresh and fragrant leaf!

Brooke, Bond's New Tea is undoubtedly the very best. Brisk, flavoury, refreshing, it's just the cup to comfortably revive and cheer you in these drowsy August days.

Will you ask our Agent, to-day, for a pound of our dainty Tea, with all its delicate bloom upon it,—tea aromatic, typic of the rich, sunlit lands of far-away Ceylon and India? We promise you it will please you. It is put up in an air-tight packet at our well-known Warehouse in the city, and, there, sealed with our celebrated trade mark of the double-triangle and also certified by our signature. So you are sure you get it just as good and just at the same price from our Agent, as if you bought it at our Headquarters. It will cost you only

1/-, 1/2, 1/4, 1/8, 2/-, 2/4, or 2/8.

BROOKE, BOND & CO. Ltd.,

THE YORKSHIRE TEA WAREHOUSES—
11, Boar Lane, and 14, White Horse Street, Leeds.
44, Kirkgate, Bradford.

By 1930 the little red vans were calling on 190,000 shops in Britain. As a result of a sales competition, sales in one week of March 1931 rose to a record 1,984,061 lbs of tea. Following on the Co-operative Society's idea of giving 'dividend' Brooke Bond started selling dividend tea in 1935, each quarter pound bearing a stamp worth 1d, each card being redeemable when filled with 60 stamps and worth 5s. This was also the decade when Pre-Gest-Te was introduced – to become much better known as 'PG Tips'. With the outbreak of the Second World War came rationing, when people were only allowed 2oz of tea per person a week.

In 1952 Gerald Brooke, the founder's son, retired and John Brooke, his son, became chairman. When Gerald took over in 1909 the company's assets were valued at £336,000 – in 1952 they were worth nearly £26 million, with operations in twelve countries and a staff of 60,000! Then came the famous picture cards, reminiscent of pre-war cigarette cards, and by 1968 720 million had been distributed. When commercial television arrived Brooke Bond became early advertisers and at Christmas time 1956 the chimpanzees made their debut in one of their advertisements. In the 1960s the first teabags were introduced and towards the end of the decade, in 1968, Brooke Bond merged with Liebig, a company with over a century of experience, involving in such well known products as Oxo and Fray Bentos.

Today it is part of Van den Bergh Foods Ltd, a subsidiary of Unilever plc.

Above: ad from the 1890s and, right, the 1950s

MARKET PLACE, WIGAN: *by William Little*

What Lancashire thinks today . . .

LANCASHIRE, although world-acknowledged county of cotton, is one of mixed industries – of coal and chemicals, glass and soap, steel, machinery, and ships. Its great port, Liverpool, is gateway to the world; its Manchester a seat of big business and true learning – and home of the Hallé Orchestra.

Lancashire folk, though schooled in materialism, are keen critics and lovers of music and the arts. Always, too, they have formed a brave front for the people's rights – as at shameful Peterloo.

Lancastrians have keen minds and powers of perception – 'What Lancashire thinks today England will think tomorrow'. They are quick to judge true worth. No wonder the little red Brooke Bond vans are kept so busy in this great Northern county. Two Brooke Bond factories are situated within its bounds.

* * *

Brooke Bond have thousands of acres of their own tea gardens – more than any other firm of tea distributors in the world – with their own buyers in all the big world tea markets. Brooke Bond is the only tea firm with five blending and packing factories in the United Kingdom. Each serves its own part of the country, and the little red vans, always a familiar sight, become more and more in evidence every week delivering fresh tea to over 150,000 shops.

Over 50 million cups of Brooke Bond tea are drunk every day

 **Brooke Bond** *good tea - and* FRESH!

We *specially* recommend

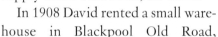

David Thomson Brown, the son of Alderman Alexander Brown, was born at New Scone in Perthshire in 1874. David's father was a potato merchant, but it was a display of prize winning onions in the window of Dickson & Turnbull in Perth, at that time Scotland's leading nurserymen and seedsmen, which at an early age fired him to want to pursue a career in horticulture.

David Brown served an apprenticeship with Dickson & Turnbull and on its completion moved to a seed-merchants in Torquay – already he had decided he also wanted to specialise in the seed trade. After this he moved to the north of England, becoming a representative for the firm of J K Yates covering the Fylde area, the Lake District and Yorkshire. By this time he was determined to start his own business, but he needed to find the right locality. During the early years of the twentieth century the hinterland of Blackpool, Marton Moss, was one of the country's main horticultural areas and David

Mr Trotter, a director of the company, and Mr Brown circa 1957

realised this was where he needed to be and so he settled in the market town of Poulton-le-Fylde, a place much visited on market days by local farmers doing business at the cattle, sheep and produce market.

Another reason for the choice of Poulton was that nearby, in Skippool, on the banks of the River Wyre, was a fertilizer company where growers came with horses and carts to buy their supplies of bone-meal; he felt sure he could also supply them with seeds, his seeds.

Brown's Poulwell

In 1908 David rented a small warehouse in Blackpool Old Road, Poulton, and from the outset determined he would only supply seed of the highest quality. Each day he went out getting orders which he made up in the evening, ready for dispatch the following morning. The business grew and soon he had to rent another warehouse on the opposite side of the road to the first one, and also employ his first assistant.

By 1920 it was necessary to move into a larger building and new premises were built in Station Road, on the site of the present offices; by now the staff had risen to fifteen. The time had now come for him to issue his retail seed catalogue, now a twice yearly event. In addition to seeds the company was also a major stockist of horticultural sundries, Dutch bulbs and garden canes, which were imported direct from China. The sourcing of seeds stretched across the world, although some were grown in the drier parts of Essex.

In about 1930 John Waddington, a retired Yorkshireman from Halifax, was taken into partnership; he wasn't a horticulturist but brought financial experience to the firm and henceforth looked after that side of the business. By 1933 the rep's standard transport was the Austin

Seven – it had no heater, lacked a good braking system and was comfortable enough providing the driver was less than six feet tall! When the reps visited the commercial growers to discuss their seed requirements, the grower would also settle up for the seeds supplied the previous season – how times have changed.

John Waddington died in 1937 and David Brown converted the firm into a limited company. That year the company purchased four acres of land and started their own trial grounds; each year tomatoes were grown under glass to produce about 50lb of seed of D T Brown's own selected strains. During those pre-war years the company grew large acreages of peas for seed in Hungary, often in conjunction with Archie Clucas, of Clucas of Ormskirk, another much respected Lancashire seed company, a friend but also a fierce competitor. D T Brown's also listed over 200 varieties of Sweet Pea, 150 varieties of cut flower Asters as well as large numbers of different Antirrhinums.

The company now expanded very rapidly and with five representatives on the road Joe Sanderson, the local representative, was made a director and came to work in the office. The Second World War disrupted the company, all the representatives being called up for military service, and whilst almost all overseas supplies of seed came to a halt still the demand for seeds grew. Importation of bulbs was prohibited and the production of flower seeds wound up; by the end of the war the flower seed trade was in a very sorry state. However, there was extra demand for edible crops, especially when the 'dig for victory' campaign encouraged households to turn their lawns into vegetable plots.

Throughout the early post-war years independent seed firms found life difficult because overseas companies, who were previously only their suppliers, now also became their competitors. There was a great demand for colour after the drab years of the war and patriotic bedding schemes of red salvia, blue lobelia and white alyssum became very popular.

Mr Brown, a lifelong bachelor, died aged 84, in 1959. He was still managing director and in the office each day, up to a few days before his death. He was a much respected man in the local community, in the seed trade, and among his staff, many of whom worked for him all their working lives.

On the death of Joe Sanderson, A V McLean, who had joined the company in 1947, became managing director, a post he held until 1994. The company is now part of Mr Fothergill's Seeds.

First warehouse, 1908

D. BYRNE & Cº

In Clitheroe, not far from the boundary between Lancashire and Yorkshire, Mr Thistlethwaite was a 'Proven' merchant in 1876. However, we are told, he was a bit of a dandy and used to enjoy riding around the town on a

large white horse. After a while he ran out of money and advertised for a partner.

Dennis Byrne's father had come over from Ireland and practised as a doctor in Salford. When he died Dennis inherited £500 and in about 1885 he came to Clitheroe looking for a business. He used the money to buy a partnership in Mr Thistlethwaite's King Street business. Within about five years his dandy partner had left the business. Around 1895 the firm became D Byrne and Company.

Dennis quickly built the business up and was soon supplying almost every farm in the Ribble Valley with cattle food, paraffin, pills for animals and even beer! He had a staff of about twenty. When he died in 1936 the business was taken over by his son George, who tended to rest on his laurels and did not develop the firm very much. Initially it was mainly reliant on

deliveries by horse and cart but as the age of the motor vehicle advanced, he ran down the delivery side and the firm became general grocers, including the sale of beers, wines and spirits.

George Michael Byrne, George's son, became involved in the shop in the mid 1950s, but did not take over fully until 1968. He saw trade moving away from the small family grocers towards the developing supermarkets and started to specialise in wine and spirits. This aspect of the business has been gradually built up since the late 1970s, and two of his sons, Philip and Andrew, joined him. He retired in 1992 and the two sons, the eldest of fourteen children, are now in partnership.

Today the shop is unchanged. It still has its original stone flagged floors, wooden counter and till. The maze of cellars, where many of the wines are stored, are in some cases under adjoining shops! But in other ways the business has marched forward, gaining its first award for excellence in 1991 – the Which? Wine Magazine's 'Best Independent Wine Merchant in Britain'; the company gained the award again in 1993. It was praised for its huge variety, enthusiasm and realistic prices.

If you want a brandy there are 50 different ones to choose from, 150 varieties of beer, 35 blends of coffee and 50 teas – at D Byrne's and Co. you are in a drinks wonderland. Other awards have come from the Wine Magazine naming the company 'Northern Wine Merchant of the Year' in 1996, 1997 and 1998. The brothers have at any one time about 3000 varieties of wine – some may cost over £100 a bottle, others no more than £3-4. Byrne's has been featured on Jancis Robinson's popular television programme 'Vintners Tales'. Whilst many locals make the shop a regular stopping place, other customers come from many miles away.

Left: metal sign from the days when the company was a proven merchant and stone jar from circa 1890 engraved Thistlethwaite and Byrne – found in a secondhand shop in Ireland. Below: Andrew Byrne raises a glass to the future with Philip Byrne (right)

Chadwick's

Apparently the making of black puddings started way back in 1810 when Casewell's made and sold them at a shop at 60 Union Street, Bury. The 'shop' was an ordinary terrace house and the black puddings were displayed on a large plate in the window; inside the house a little table acted as a counter. This shop remained in existence until 1965.

Another Bury black pudding maker was Joshua Thompson, a brawny Cumberland wrestler, who in 1865 made them in the cellar of his house in the Mosses part of Bury. He later moved to a shop in East Street. Eventually his great-grandson, Harry Reddish, started selling black puddings on Bury Market along its Moss Street frontage in 1929, and ran the stall until his death 43 years later. His nephew Kenneth Young inherited the stall, but then it was taken over by Edwin (Eddie) Chadwick.

Edwin Chadwick started as a butcher, in 1971, in premises at 247 Burnley Road East, Waterfoot.

Busy as usual on the stall at Bury market.

At that time selling black puddings was just a side line, along with bacon and sausages and all the other savouries found in a typical butcher's shop. Local people soon appreciated the quality of Edwin's black puddings and the demand for them increased.

In 1972 the opportunity came for him to take over the black pudding stall on Bury Market, and once again the trade grew and grew. By 1974 the trade in black puddings had grown so large and time consuming that he decided to close the butchering side of the business. Over the years customers have included personalities such as Ken Dodd, Julie Goodyear and Pat Phoenix.

There are even World Championships, which are held at Corner Pin, a pub in Ramsbottom. Yorkshire puddings are placed in a row and contestants from all over the world throw a black pudding at them – the feud it seems goes on!.

Edwin's daughter Mary (who started helping her father when she was only six) and her husband, Tony Sinacola now make 1 1/2 to 2 tons of black puddings a week, supplying hotels, restaurants and wholesale butchers. Although basically black puddings are made of pig's blood, barley, oatmeal, pork fat, rusk and herbs, the actual recipe is a secret known only to Mary and Tony.

In 1998 thirteen contestants took their places in Bury's Sir Robert Peel's pub for a black pudding eating contest; the winner, Martin Brimelow, managed to eat nine of the succulent delicacy!

In December 1998 Chadwicks made a huge black pudding for their favourite charity, the Bury Hospice – it was over 40 feet long, weighed over 115 lbs and lay in a basket like a huge coiled black snake!

Black Puddings were probably made in many parts of the country in Victorian times, and even in France and Germany. Today, they are exported to Saudi Arabia, Australia and Canada. But why they should be so strongly linked with Bury remains a mystery.

Mary Chadwick with the monster pudding which raised money for the Bury Hospice.

It would seem inconceivable to write a book about Lancashire businesses and not mention the Co-operative Movement, for the present day Co-operative Societies saw their birth in Rochdale.

However, the spirit of co-operation existed in Lancashire long before the Rochdale Pioneers. John Finch, born in Dudley in 1784, arrived in Liverpool in 1818. He became a successful businessman in the city and in 1839 established the Hall of Science in Lord Nelson Street. He saw co-operation as a way of life, bringing people together not only as consumers, but also to learn and socialise.

The Rochdale Pioneers got their inspiration from Robert Owen, a Welshman, who had become managing director of a large spinning mill in New Lanark, Scotland. He had a vision of a new society based on co-operation, or socialism as it was known by his followers – it called for a sense of brotherhood rather than following selfish ways. It was in 1841 that Owenites became known as Socialists.

The Rochdale Society of Equitable Pioneers established their society on 15 August 1844. They opened for business on 21 December at their 'shop' in Toad Lane – the ground floor of an old warehouse, underneath a chapel, but it was only rented! Their opening hours were from 8pm to 10pm on two evenings a week. Initially they had little money and therefore the stock was limited to butter, sugar, flour, oatmeal and candles.

There were 28 original Pioneers, and they included weavers, a shoemaker, a block-printer, a hatter and a hawker. Starting a business was one thing, keeping their customers faithful to the concept was more difficult. Charles Howarth, a warper in a cotton mill, suggested that the profits be divided among the members in proportion to the amount they spent – this became known as the 'dividend'; the money accumulated in this way was often used by the members to buy shoes and other essential items for their children.

New members had to be proposed and seconded by two members. By 1849 they had 390 members and their capital sum had risen to £1,193. The Society's first branch was opened in Oldham Road, Rochdale in 1856 and others soon followed.

The Society in Oldham itself started in 1850. At this time Oldham had a population of about 50,000 and had just been created a body corporate. The majority of the inhabitants had little food, clothing or shelter – many lived in alleys, or cellars which were neither drained nor ventilated. Their working hours were long, wages low and education was almost non-existent for the working classes – however, there was 'much tippling, dog-racing and pigeon flying'! Many weavers were earning only one shilling a week.

The initial meeting took place in Braddock's Buildings, and although not a success, it led to a second effort which produced a Society beyond the founders' wildest dreams, the Oldham Equitable Co-operative Society, initially known as the Greenacres Hill Industrial Co-operative Society. At this latter meeting on

No. 2 BRANCH, 150, BUTLER STREET, ANCOATS.

a November evening at the home of William Turton in Kershaw Place, the six working men emptied their pockets of what money they had, which amounted to 15s. They took this to the wholesale shop of Mr Marsden, at Bottom-o'-th'-Moor, opposite the Black Swan, and purchased various groceries including tea, coffee, and sugar – each member then took home their share, according to the amount of capital they had subscribed.

Early in 1851 the Committee decided to place the Society on a more business-like footing, seeking shop premises. One of the founders, John Taylor, offered them his house in Derker Street and from this cottage they sold tea, sugar and spices, not having room to store other items. Later in the year they moved into a shop at 130 Huddersfield Road and their range of goods increased – in December they purchased half a cow and a sheep!

However, early in 1852 Mr Turton asked to be relieved of his duties as treasurer as both he and his wife worked at the mill throughout the day and the cashbox had to be left at home, which they felt was not a safe place!

By this time the Society had 100 members, but the shop was only open during the evening; officers of the Society served their fellow members without any payment, knowing only that they had been helping each other.

Another Society which started in a similar way was the Great and Little Bolton one. Again the people lived on a meagre diet, often only porridge, and wanting to improve their lot, they sent a deputation to Rochdale to see whether co-operation would work in Bolton. The group came back convinced that it could, and they preached co-operation to everyone they met.

Meetings were held at the home of Thomas Ashton, a beerhouse in Derby Street, and he became the first registered member and also the treasurer. Unfortunately he died before the first shop was opened, but his wife 'Gladdy' Ashton took on his role, a position she held for many years. Gladdy Ashton offered the Society their first shop, one next to her beerhouse, on the understanding that if the shop was successful they would pay the usual rent, but if not then no rent would be payable, and that would be all right – they were given a 14 year lease at £14 per year. Women played a leading role in the development of the Society.

The first subscriptions were 3d a week, or 3s 3d a quarter, each one pledging to pay this until he had £5 standing to his credit; he was then considered a full member. In August 1859 a code of rules was adopted and the Society became registered as the 'Great and Little Bolton Equitable Industrial Co-operative Society

Limited'. However, being cautious people they did not trade under this name but under the name of Jos. Bridge, a millworker. For a short time it only opened from 6pm to 10pm, when work at the factories had stopped. Bread was fetched in clothes baskets from a local baker's. Other members went to the wholesalers to purchase a variety of goods, but no time was as lively as when pigs were brought to the shop, were killed, cut up and distributed to the vari-

ous members who had previously placed their orders for particular parts of the animals.

Many local shopkeepers were far from sympathetic to their new competitors and did everything they could to bring discredit to the movement. Eventually the Co-op made arrangements with other shops in the town to supply goods that the Society did not sell, a percentage of these sales going to the Society, and the member getting credit for the amount spent.

The Accrington Society was begun by a group of weavers meeting together but it was not registered until 1860. However, before that time these weavers had been practising a system of co-operative buying.

However, not everything was about business, for the Societies also took an interest in education and social activities. At Bolton a party was held on New Year's Day at the Baths and this was followed by an all night dance, with musical accompaniment from a reed band – one of

the members of the Society used to teach the members to dance in the Reading Room, after it had closed for the day, this time accompanied by a concertina and fiddle!

There were also 'Smoking Concerts', but only men aged over 21 were allowed to attend these; separate concerts were held for ladies, and there were also singing classes.

To meet the needs of this growing army of Societies, the Co-operative Wholesale Society was begun in 1863 in a small warehouse in Manchester. In 1869 the C W S built its own premises in Balloon Street, Manchester which housed a varied range of departments including the Co-operative Bank, Furnishing and Stationery Departments, Grocery Saleroom (supplying 100 tons of self-raising flour each week, as well as tapioca, rice, linseed, oatmeal and canary seed), buyers' offices, and the Shoe Department (holding 220,000 pairs of shoes). Within a decade they were manufacturing their own goods.

The Women's Co-operative Guild was founded in 1883 – its aim was to educate women in the principles of co-operation.

The Liverpool Equitable Co-operative Society came into being in 1886, giving the co-operative movement in the city a renewed firm footing and so the flame of Co-operation has spread throughout the land and across the world. Today there are supermarkets in almost all the main towns and cities of Britain, and in the smaller communities and suburbs the Co-op is seen as a valuable part of the community.

Many of the principles of those Rochdale Pioneers are still embraced in the movement today.

KEEPS GOOD SHOES·GOOD SHOES

Not far from Clitheroe Castle, at the top of Castle Street, is a butcher's shop – Cowman's. The building is old, the front about 200 years, whilst the rear portion may be 400 years old, with parts even dating back to the 12th century. The rear wall is solid rock, but this only came to light in 1972 when Edward Cowburn, whose family now own the shop, cleared away the old uneven plaster to build a new wall.

Cowman's have a long association with Clitheroe, being both farmers and butchers, originally having a butcher's shop in Lowergate. Thomas Cowman had a butcher's shop in Parson Lane but in 1880 he bought the shop, 13 Castle Street, from John Kendal. For over thirty years he also had a stall under one of the windows of the Swan Hotel, when the weekly market was held in the main street.

John Cowman was born in 1851 and he also joined the family business. In 1893 the business was taken over by John and his brother James. John became well known in the Manchester and northern cattle markets, and before the construction of the railway to Settle he regularly drove the sheep he had purchased along the 18 miles of highway between Settle and Clitheroe. In those days, and into the 20th century, Cowman's only closed during Wakes Week, and then only from Saturday morning

to Thursday morning. Just before Christmas live turkeys would come to Clitheroe by train and would then be walked up King Street to the Castle Street premises.

John Cowman used to select and roast the oxen at such occasions of public rejoicing as the Golden and Diamond Jubilees of Queen Victoria, and at the Coronation of Edward VII. He also served on the Town Council for about twenty years as councillor and alderman, becoming chairman of the Cattle Market and Farm and Sewerage Committees. John and his wife Mary Ann had five sons and eight daughters.

While John was on one of his regular visits to Appleby market one day in 1925 he had a heart attack, and fell badly. He was sent home by taxi but he died the following day. The firm now

Castle Street in Clitheroe where Cowman's started and still operates

Left: the Ox Roasting Committee at Castle Fete and, below, roasting an ox at the coronation celebrations of Edward VII in Clitheroe in 1911. Ox roasters are pictured on page 55.

became Cowman Bros., and in the 1930s and 1940s four members of the family had butcher's shops in Clitheroe – James (Jim) had one in Eshton Terrace, and John one in Wellgate; Bobbie, before taking over the Castle Street shop, had one at 61 Whalley Road and Richard had the Castle Street shop before that. Nellie and Lizzie were confectioners in King Street.

Because most of the sons were either childless, or had only girls, there was no logical successor to take over the business in the late 1950s. It had short periods when it became Taylor & Jones, and then Whitham's. In 1960 Edward (Ted) Cowburn became the shop manager, having been in partnership with his father and brother as butchers. In 1961 he bought the business and restored the name 'Cowman'. Thus a long tradition was reinstated. . . it helped that the name was so much like that of his own family.

Today Cowman's butcher's shop is run by Cliff Cowburn, himself a fifth generation butcher and Ted's son. It is best known for its wide range of different flavoured sausages – nearly 60 varieties ranging from Rosemary Lamb, Pork and Orange, Pork, Apple and Mint to Venison and Wild Boar. In 1994 The Times Magazine listed Clitheroe in its top ten towns for specialist shopping, giving mention to Cowman's Famous Sausage Shop – no mean accolade!

Cliff Cowburn

Lancashire Cheese has been made for centuries, but it wasn't until late in the 18th Century that the unique 'Lancashire system' became established. As much of the cheese was made in farmhouses, and many farms would only have a small amount of curd each day, curds saved over three days were mixed together. This was known as the three day curd system – which gives a distinctive buttery mellow cheese. Small scale production continued in hundreds of small dairies and farmhouse kitchens, for it was a profitable way of using excess milk, which has a short shelf life but when converted into cheese will last for several months.

Cheesemaking was a skilful and demanding work – it involved lifting heavy pails of milk and water, working in damp conditions, pressing, cutting and lifting curd and finished cheeses, which weighed 40 lbs. There was an old saying: 'The bigger the dairymaid, the better the cheese!' There were cheese competitions at Goosnargh and Garstang where cheesemakers showed their skills, but some farm cheesemaking was poor, so eventually Lancashire County Council decided to finance a programme of technical education in farming, and to include cheesemaking. By 1894 Hutton Hall near Preston had been chosen as the site for the Agricultural College. One of the peripatetic teachers who went out to instruct and help cheesemakers was Joseph Gornall.

Joseph Gornall is perhaps the most important name in the story of Lancashire cheesemaking. He came from a background of farming and cheesemaking and offered practical help and advice based on real life experience, and was able to work with the farming community. The service of the Cheese Instructor was free of charge, providing the farmer offered board and lodging for the instructor, and allowed as many people as could be reasonably accommodated in the farmhouse to watch the teacher at work. Joseph used to say 'that if every cheesemaker in Lancashire would be determined to make nothing but fine, free mellow cheese of good flavour, we should not need to fear any competition with Cheshires, or American cheeses'. He also designed cheesemaking equipment, including Gornall's Patent Cheesemaker. He lived and farmed at Clay Lane Head Farm, Cabus, near Garstang, only a few miles from where George Kenyon founded Dew-Lay Cheeses many years later.

George Kenyon had always worked in the cheese industry – he worked at Grimshaw & Culshaw at Scorton as a wagon driver, but later moved to Palatine Dairies at Blackburn as manager. He thought about starting his own business but lacked the necessary capital. However, one day he had a motor cycle accident on his BSA Bantam, and using the insurance money he opened for business on Green Lane, Cabus (near where Joseph Gornall used to be) in April 1957.

The name Dew-Lay came from the French 'Du lait', meaning 'from the milk', but as George came from Wigan rather than France his was an unintentional misspelling and mispronunciation. George was a very strict taskmaster but he set the company off with the same objectives it has today, ensuring that its products are of the highest quality. He came to work almost every day, but sadly died in 1995, two years before Dew-Lay moved to their new dairy.

On the outskirts of Garstang the company has a building constructed to the highest standards – it includes air conditioning, filtered air, controlled temperatures, positive air pressures and many other pieces of sophisticated equipment to ensure the highest standards of food safety and good working conditions for the staff, to still make handcrafted cheeses.

When the company moved its processing plant they brought with them the 'mother culture', which is the bacteria used to make the cheese. Dew-Lay have been using the same culture for over 25 years. A small amount is saved every day and used again to make starter for the following day's cheese-making.

In recent years the company, under the management of Neil and John Kenyon, George Kenyon's sons, has developed links with some of the major supermarkets producing their own brand cheeses as well as Dew-Lay's renowned own label cheese. One unusual line for which the company is becoming well known is kosher cheese, originally for the Jewish community, but now enjoyed by a wider clientele. Its production has to be carefully monitored, and many of the resultant cheeses go to consumers in London and Manchester.

The company still produces many traditional 40 lb round cheeses. Dew-Lay feel that it is likely in the next few years, due to the demise of the small shopkeeper and market stalls, and the increase in convenience shopping, that the trend towards prepacked cheeses will increase and with this in mind have invested in high tech prepacking equipment.

Lancashire cheese is a good cheese both for freezing and melting. Dew-Lay produce a wide variety of traditional cheeses, ranging from Creamy Lancashire, Tasty Lancashire to Lancashire with additives, garlic, chives and more.

To begin with all the cooking was done in Mary's kitchen, Fred taking the jars of jam on a handcart to the Co-operative Store. Soon the business was so successful that they ran out of storage space and in 1884 Fred purchased a house, which had a small warehouse attached to it, in Audenshaw Road, Guide Bridge, North Manchester. However, this proved an unwieldy arrangement so that same year he raised sufficient capital to allow him to build and equip his own factory in Deanhead, Guide Bridge.

Fred Duerr was born in London, not far from Tower Bridge, the son of George and Jemima Duerr. George and his father were both leather dressers, but Fred chose not to follow in their footsteps.

Fred's parents moved to live in Bristol and then to Northampton, a centre for the shoe industry, but in 1872 Fred, now 24 years old, married 16 year old Mary Eva Naylor in Leeds. They made their first home at 2 Barnfield Street in Heywood, near Rochdale and in 1877 the first of their three sons, Oliver, was born there. At that time Fred was a commercial traveller, later becoming a grocery commission agent.

By 1881 Fred and Mary were living at Moss Cottage, off Bamford Road, in Heywood.

That year Fred met Honest John Butterworth, the buyer for Heywood Co-operative Society, who complained that he was unable to buy preserves of sufficiently high quality, many of them containing unacceptable additives. (The original Rochdale Equitable Pioneers, the founding fathers of the Co-operative movement, had as one of their principles:'Pure food at reasonable prices, not adulterated'.) He went on to ask Fred if his wife, whose jam making skills were legendary throughout the locality, would consider making jams to supply to the Co-operative Society — he promised to take all she could make!

The Century's Progress in 1890 recorded '[The works] are admirably situated in a fine open stretch of country, between Manchester and Ashton, and they rank among the most complete works of the kind in the country. The principal building is of ample size, and every part is filled up in a thorough style, with plant and apparatus of the latest and most improved description...The boiling house is on the first floor, and is a spacious and well-

Fred Duerr and his wife
Mary Eva who started it all

appointed department in which a number of copper preserve pans are in constant use. After each boiling the result is carefully tested, and then forwarded by a species of miniature tram service to the making up and labelling rooms...Mr Duerr is well known for his superior skill in selecting fruit of the proper nature, and for sound judgement as to the precise time when the fruit is at its best for preserving. All the fruit is chosen by the proprietor – it is hand-picked and is of the most suitable quality only. Every process is carefully watched and is carried out by experienced persons with the best possible appliances.'

Fred Duerr and his business were soon successful. He became a member of the Corn Exchange, attending every Tuesday, and attributed his achievement to careful fruit buying and the application of scientific principles to jam making. He claimed that his secret method of fruit preservation enabled his preserves to keep longer without deteriorating – this was important for he would generally have in store some 35,000 one gallon jars of fruit for use during the winter months.

About this time the Duerrs moved to Talbot Road, Old Trafford. Subsequent homes were then The Haven, Stanley Road, Whalley Range; then Oak Road, Old Trafford before they retired to Lytham St. Anne's. There was also a need to move the business as the premises in Guide Bridge were not large enough to meet the demand, and in 1893 Fred had a new factory built in Prestage Street, Old Trafford at a cost of £1,315 16s 4d. This was a considerable investment for those days, and did not include the cost of the manufacturing equipment.

As far back as 1905, when many of their competitors were still using cardboard caps for their jars, Fred Duerr had pioneered vacuum sealing jars – he claimed 'The natural flavour of the fruit is retained to a remarkable degree by a process used exclusively by us'. The process preserved the fruit's natural colour and allowed the jam to be kept indefinitely.

Oliver, Edgar and Alfred, the three sons of Fred and Mary, joined the company in the early years of the new century. Alfred built up sales, particularly by concentrating on the many Co-operative Societies in North West England. During the Boer War the company had sent out tins of jam to the Lancashire Fusiliers, but in the First World War Edgar Duerr branched out to invent a pocket collapsible periscope which was widely used by soldiers in the trench warfare; one of these is on display in the Imperial War Museum in London.

Fred had worked hard for his success, coming from very humble beginnings. He was a sober and careful man who wanted to ensure that those who benefited from his industry would not waste what was to be theirs. In 1906 he wrote to one of his nephews that he was bequeathing him £500 in his will, providing he did not 'drink, gamble or do any other foolish things'.

It wasn't unusual for whole families to work for Duerr's, and many people spent their whole working life with the company – indeed Emily Deakin started at the age of 14 and stayed until she was 74! Staff received half yearly bonuses and were paid good wages compared to similar workers in other firms. The Duerr family were all very much involved with the company.

In the 1920s and 30s the company ran one of their most successful promotions; it called upon customers to collect 20 Duerr's labels and in return they received a copy of a colourful fruit picture – further copies were available at 5s each. The cherries in the picture were actually some that had been on Granny Duerr's hat, cherries not being in season at the time!

F Duerr & Sons became a limited company in 1924 and by 1935 Oliver's sons, Norman and Clive Duerr, had taken over the running of the business. They saw the company through the difficult years of the Second World War when sugar and other raw materials were in short supply, skilled workers were conscripted to the armed forces and it was difficult to get parts for the machinery. After the war Harry Duerr became a familiar face in Manchester's Smithfeld Market, often being there at 4

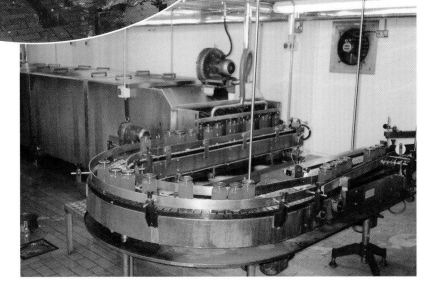

Right: a modern jam production line at Floats Road helps the company meet the many varied demands of customers.
Above: the old jam production area.
Left: back of a 1914 price list and examples from the Duerr archive including, centre bottom of picture, a pair of vacuum sealed jars from 1903 in which the jam should still be edible!

o'clock in the morning selecting the best of the fruit, or similarly he could be found at 8 o'clock at night in the middle of a fruit field in Evesham watching fruit being loaded onto wagons, destined for Manchester the following morning.

Edgar Duerr had been chairman of the company until his death, at the age of 82, in 1962. He was succeeded by Oliver's son, Norman, but sadly he died two years later at the early age of 57. After this Jim Harrison, the husband of Edgar's daughter, Alma, was appointed non executive chairman and Tony Duerr, Norman's son, was appointed managing director at the age of 27.

The early 60s were difficult years as some of Duerr's major customers regrouped their businesses, forming companies such as Spar, Mace and VG. Duerr's lost a lot of wholesale distribution at that time but regained ground when they won a large contract to pack VG 'own brand' preserves. Later, in the early 1970s, further progress was made when Kwik Save shops started to stock Duerr Preserves, thereby introducing the brand to customers

Chairman Tony Duerr is greeted by Her Majesty the Queen in 1995 when he is awarded an OBE for "Services to the Food Industry".

across the country.

Today Tony Duerr OBE is chairman, with his sons Mark and Richard holding important positions in the company. It is now one of the country's three largest jam manufacturers and the largest independent one with 20 per cent of the United Kingdom market. The new production line for peanut butter, only started in 1989, now accounts for 30 per cent of all UK sales of peanut butter. Duerr's major customers are now the large multiple supermarkets who sell its products both as Duerr Preserves and as 'own brands'. It now also exports to over fifteen countries, from Australia to Singapore, Denmark to China.

In 1995 Duerr's new 70,000 sq ft Floats Road complex at Wythenshawe was opened; in 1997 they commissioned a £300,000 marmalade advertising campaign – and also celebrated having produced a hundred million jars of preserve since they began in Mary's kitchen way back in 1881!

GRANADA TELEVISION

The beginnings of the North West's independent television station go back many years to the enterprise of Alexander Bernstein who opened the Edmonton Empire Music Hall in 1908. This was the family's first venture into the world of showbusiness, following in the spirit of Phineas Taylor Barnum the great American man of 'showbusiness'.

Sidney Bernstein, Alexander's second son, was born in 1899. During the spring of 1920, while on a walking holiday in Spain, he arrived one snowy night in the city of Granada. The snow melted early next day and he discovered the wonder of Granada, with its ancient and magnificent Alhambra, the palace, started in 1238. At that time he was seeking a new name for their theatres – 'Granada' captured that exotic theatrical feel he was seeking. The first two cinemas to follow this dream were the Granada at Dover and the Granada at Walthamstow. The Tooting theatre re-opened

as the 'most luxurious bingo club in the world', and from the 1960s such Bingo Social Clubs became a major part of the Granada Theatre group.

By 1930 Sidney had become involved at the Royal Court and Phoenix Theatres in London. Sidney had seen America's palatial new cinema houses and this encouraged him to build entirely new style cinemas in Britain. They were masterpieces of elegance, but he also managed them in innovative ways.

Lord Bernstein

During the years of the Second World War Granada cinemas provided a refuge from the bombs, and audiences were entertained throughout the night with films, organ music, and community singing.

In 1964 Granada opened its first motorway service station at Toddington on the M1, and over the next few years sites were developed throughout the country, each with restaurants, shops and petrol stations.

Viewing television is now accepted as an important part of life, but back in the 1960s when reception was often poor, a number of firms provided a TV cable relay system, and also rented sets to their users. By 1964 Granada had built up a chain of about 200 rental shops, but the coming of colour television gave Granada TV Rental an opportunity to expand further. In 1970 Britain only had 100,000 colour TV sets but by 1978 this had grown to twelve million. By 1984 Granada had become the largest rental chain in the country.

However, Granada's move into providing a television network goes back to 1948. Sidney and his brother Cecil had applied for a licence for a close television circuit which would allow them to film West End shows on the last night of their run and then show them for one night on their large cinema screens – they were turned down! The Television Act he had helped to formulate received the Royal Assent in 1954, and the Independent Television Authority was set up. On 25 August the ITA sought applications from people who wished to become programme contractors. This time they bid for the Northern Region and were successful; they had a licence to operate five days a week although they had hoped for seven. Sidney Bernstein said that his reason for choosing this region, and not the south, came about by looking at two maps – one was density of population, the other was rainfall! The ITA stated that it was looking for companies that could produce high quality balanced programmes over a long period.

A wholly owned subsidiary company, Granada Television Ltd, was formed which later became Granada TV Network Ltd; it was one of the four founding independent television network companies and was the first to create a purpose built centre. The ITA had determined that the companies could not operate centrally from London. Sidney chose a derelict site in the heart of Manchester – his television centre would be at the heart of the people it sought to serve. He chose Ralph Tubbs to design it; he had been the architect of the Dome of Discovery at the Festival of Britain in 1951.

Staff had to be trained to become directors, producers, vision mixers, assistants – for anything from a musical to a panel game. Sidney addressed them personally, reassured them, and then sent them to Manchester to be trained on the 'Travelling Eyes', which were to be their outside broadcast units, covering sports fixtures and other important events; they also provided good publicity for Granada during this important run-up period. By now Sidney and Cecil Bernstein had identified their respective roles in the organisation. They kept to them, and until Cecil's death in 1981 they had a good relationship.

The company had shown the wide variety of interests they intended to present, and among these was classical music. To ensure good standards they asked Sir Thomas Beecham to become their musical consultant – whilst he agreed he also suggested that they should include opera, ballet, and works from less popular composers; he also stated his fee, and

Brian Inglis presents the first edition of What the Papers Say in 1956 and (right) the first live TV coverage of an election campaign in February 1958

Granada accepted.

Transmitters were built at Winter Hill and Emley Moor so that both Lancashire and Yorkshire could be serviced independently; the first Lancashire transmission commenced at 7.30pm on 3 May 1956. Yorkshire had to wait until November. London viewing figures, however, were not realising their anticipated levels, advertisers were pulling out, and the scene was a gloomy one. From the beginning the companies had to provide programmes eight hours a day, a very heavy commitment especially if much of it was to be live entertainment.

Unlike the other independent stations, Sidney did not intend the opening ceremony to be a 'white tie' event, but one which reflected its future content, and Granada's 'constituency'. The programmes in those early weeks and months included foreign films, but also material 'networked' from the other companies, as well as the outside broadcasts, and four programmes which were to become family favourites for many years – 'Youth is Asking' where well known people were questioned by young people, 'My Wildest Dream' which was a panel game, 'Spot the Tune' a musical quiz, and 'Zoo Time' a forerunner of many animal programmes. The outside broadcasts included pictures of local traffic bottlenecks, the triumphant homecoming of the Manchester City football team with the cup after their visit to Wembley, and an interview with L S Lowry.

The gloomy financial situation of the other ITV companies now started to bite at Granada as losses averaged £20,000 a week. Sidney Bernstein had to personally go out and meet with chairmen of some of the most powerful household commodity companies and seek their promise of advertising

slots during this early period, offering benefits to them in future months. He was a very persuasive man and within a short time had agreements from such companies as Colgate, Lever Brothers and Beecham's. Additionally, networking increased, at previously set rates, between the various independent television companies, and other less public deals gave Granada some access to London audiences. However, within months it became clear that commercial television was going to be both popular and a financial success.

Granada was the first to break the news of President Kennedy's assassination, and of Macmillan's resignation as Prime Minister.

Since 1967 Granada Television has provided television seven days a week to people in Greater Manchester, Merseyside, Lancashire, Cheshire and adjoining counties.

Coronation Street, one of the network's most successful programmes, began on 9 December 1960, but was not initially accepted by other networks on the grounds that it was too parochial! Not only has it since achieved vast viewing figures in this country, but is now enjoyed in many countries throughout the world. Even Her Majesty the Queen has visited 'The Street', coming to the Granada Centre in 1982.

From its earliest days the network has encouraged the arts, including classical music and ballet. In 1960 it screened a 75 minute production of Cinderella, featuring Margot Fonteyn, Michael Somes and the Royal Ballet Company; in 1982 Granada was awarded the International Emmy in the Performing Arts for A Lot of Happiness, again with the Royal Ballet Company, which traced the creation of a ballet by the choreographer. Drama has also been well represented by such programmes as Brideshead Revisited and The Jewel in the Crown.

Other programmes which have attracted large viewing figures include live sporting events, current affairs, children's programmes, and regular contests, such as University Challenge and The Krypton Factor.

In 1969 Sidney Bernstein was granted a Life Peerage; ten years later Lord Berstein of Leigh became President of the Granada Group.

Sir Kenneth Clark (later Lord Clark), former chairman of ITA, wrote in 1958: 'We did not quite foresee how much Granada would develop a character which distinguishes it most markedly from the other programme companies and from the BBC. This character may be described as immediacy – Granada believes in today.' Later, in 1984, The Economist wrote: 'Alone among the commercial companies, Granada has vigorously maintained not just a creditable current affairs output but a strong innovative tradition, including staged cabinet reconstructions and one-off investigative programmes.'

Probably Granada TV's most famous export – 'The Street', visited here by Her Majesty the Queen in 1982

Granada still believes in today and today's world, but also focuses keenly on the future. Its hotel brands, including Heritage and Post House, are household names, and the motorway service stations, TV rental business and roadside restaurants (including Little Chef) go from strength to strength. Television is now going through an unprecedented period of development and growth, and the company's media division (Granada Media) is very much part of this. It has invested in a number of other UK broadcasters, launched several satellite channels, and is at the forefront of the digital revolution. Today, an international company with offshoots in the US and Australia, it makes new programmes for both the domestic and international markets.

Granada Media continues to challenge issues which are current or affect our future, but also knows it must inform and entertain, and in doing so, contribute to the fulness of life – especially in the North West.

*The*Guardian

John Edward Taylor was aquitted at Lancaster Assizes of criminally libelling John Greenwood, the Manchester Tory Leader, on 30 March 1819. As Taylor travelled back to Manchester in a coach, accompanied by John Childs, a printer from Bungay in Suffolk, Childs suggested to him that he should start a newspaper. The Guardian, or as it was known and loved for many years, the Manchester Guardian, traces its origin to this meeting.

John Edward Taylor was born in 1791, the son of a Presbyterian minister, who had become a Quaker. For many years his father was headmaster of a

John Edward Taylor

Quaker school in Manchester, but although John became a pupil there, he also received lessons in mathematics from John Dalton.

On leaving school Taylor was apprenticed to Benjamin Oakden, a cotton manufacturer, and later he became a partner in the business, before becoming a merchant. However, he had more interest in public life than in business and he became secretary of a school in Lancaster which offered education to the working classes.

In political terms Taylor was a reformer, a dangerous stand to take in those times. In 1813 a friend took him to meet Leigh Hunt in Horsemanger Lane prison; Hunt had been imprisoned for two years for libelling the Prince Regent, but while there, he was editing the Examiner from his cell.

This impressed Taylor, who was still only 21 years old, and he, and Archibald Prentice, sub-

sequently started writing political articles for the Manchester Gazette.

At this time neither Manchester nor Salford had a town council but had a number of committees, each for a specific purpose. In 1818 the police commissioners wanted to appoint Taylor as an assessor for Salford, but John Greenwood objected and Taylor was not appointed.

1819 saw political unrest in the manufacturing areas of the Midlands and North of England; revolution was in the air. At that time neither the merchants nor the manufacturers had representation in parliament and the ordinary workers had no votes at all. As a result of this tension a meeting was called in Manchester's St Peter's Fields at which the speaker was Henry Hunt, a popular orator of the day. The magistrates called out the special constables, the cavalry and the yeomanry – the subsequent mayhem became known as 'Peterloo', such was the bloodshed. The event was well covered in the newspapers and an article prepared by either Taylor or Prentice reached the London-based Times ahead of that of their own reporter, John Tyas. They were determined that they would tell the true story, afraid that the magistrate's report to the Home Office might not be so accurate! Their telling of the death of eleven people and the wounding of hundreds made sensational news and gave the event national attention, something it might otherwise not have had.

Afterwards Taylor carefully compiled his Notes and Observations and offered a rational, reliable account with the minimum of passion and moral anger. He and other reformers realised that they needed a powerful newspaper and in the end Taylor decided to start a new one himself. His friends provided the financial backing; he and Prentice had the literary expertise. The arrangement was that ten men put up £100 and an eleventh put up £50. The money was to be repaid when the paper was in a position to do so, but if it failed there was to be no claim against Taylor. He was not only editor but also sole proprietor.

A prospectus told of the forthcoming publication on Saturday, 5th of May 1821 of 'No. 1 of a New Weekly Paper to be entitled The Manchester Guardian', price 7d:

'The MANCHESTER GUARDIAN will commence its course with a very considerable circulation. It has secured an extensive and valuable patronage throughout the surrounding districts, among the classes to whom, more especially, Advertisements are generally addressed; and whilst its Conductors respectfully solicit the support of advertisers both in this and the neighbouring towns, they confidently assure them, that it will offer a most eligible medium for giving extensive publicity to their notices.'

Those reading the Prospectus were also told that it would support a consistent character 'for sincere and undeviating attachment to rational Liberty. . . It will zealously enforce the principles of civil and religious Liberty, the most comprehensive sense of those terms; it will warmly advocate the cause of Reform; it will endeavour to assist in the diffusion of just principles of Political Economy.' It was also going to report on Parliamentary and public debates, foreign matters, and trade, with of course particular

emphasis on the cotton industry.

Its first home was in rented premises at 29 Market Street for which they paid £31. 10s a year. That first issue very much mirrored the intentions set out in the prospectus, for it contained articles on gold and currency, tainted police evidence, European news, the grain markets of Liverpool and London, and also featured a long list of bankruptcies.

The Manchester Guardian was a weekly paper for its first fifteen years; then it was published 'half-weekly', before becoming a daily paper in 1855 when the price was reduced to 2d when Stamp Duty was lifted – it had been regarded as a tax on knowledge!

John Edward Taylor, the founder, married his cousin Sophia Russell Scott, whose nephew C P (Charles Prestwich) Scott eventually became the paper's editor for 60 years. Between 1821 and 1870 the paper was essentially run by members of the Taylor family but by the late 1860s John Taylor's son, Edward, wanted to give up the editorship. Through family connections C P

'The Battle of Peterloo' in Manchester's St Peter's Fields, 1819

The current offices in Deansgate, left, with the Cross Street offices above

Scott, then a student at Oxford, was recommended to him and joined the paper in 1871. Early the following year, while only 26, he became editor and in 1907 he became proprietor.

During the whole of his editorship he continued to emphasise liberal politics, but also opposed the worst excesses of colonialism, particularly in Sudan and South Africa. He supported home rule for Ireland, the Zionist cause and the proposal for a Jewish state.

C P Scott died in 1932, having been editor for 50 years, and for many years also proprietor. The ownership passed to his two sons, John Scott and Edward Scott, but when Edward died that same year John Scott became aware of the devastating effects death duties would have if he, as sole owner, were also to die. To prevent this happening he transferred all his shares, and

the benefits from them, into the hands of trustees, the Trust becoming the owners of the Manchester Guardian and Manchester Evening News.

As early as 1944 Laurence Scott, grandson of C P Scott, had laid down three essentials for the future of the paper – firstly that the front page should contain news, rather than advertisements, secondly that 'Manchester' be dropped from the title, and thirdly that the paper be distributed from London as well as Manchester. The front page wasn't changed until 1952, and the name not until 1959; moreover 'The Guardian' wasn't printed in London until 1961!

During the editorship of Alastair Hetherington (1956-75) the paper strongly opposed the Suez invasion, a stance which, unpopular at the time, proved creditable in later years.

To enable The Guardian to secure lucrative national advertising from large companies it was felt essential that the paper should have at least a presence in London. There was great reluctance to leave their 'mother city' but the London office was increased in size and some pages of each day's paper were produced in each city and then brought together to form a complete newspaper. However, the editor began to feel increasingly detached from the affairs of Government and in 1964 the paper's editorial headquarters moved to London, although they still retained their Manchester office and continued to print there. In 1970 the office transferred from Cross Street to a new building at 164 Deansgate, still in the heart of Manchester.

The paper failed to win the sought-after advertising and a financial crisis loomed – there was even talk of a merger with The Times. Alastair Hetherington strongly opposed this and won the day, and happily the paper was steered to a stronger future by chairman Peter Gibbings and by Peter Preston when he became

First issue, 1521, with today's masthead

In 1987 a new Print Centre in London's Dockland's Isle of Dogs was opened. The following year a newly designed two section Guardian arrived at the newsagents, followed by the Weekend Guardian and the Guardian International, which is produced in and for Europe.

In more recent times the paper, under the editorship of Peter Preston, and his successor Alan Rusbridger, has continued to crusade as did John Taylor all those years ago. The Guardian has held true to its mandate.

Over the years many people have flexed their professional muscles on The Guardian – Arthur Ransome, Alistair Cooke, Neville Cardus, Malcolm Muggeridge, Bernard Ingham, Bernard Levin and Salman Rushdie to name but a few. Commercially the Manchester Guardian had to move to London, but its roots will always be seen as having been laid down in Manchester, foundations strong and true which have allowed the paper to grow, prosper, and endure in the cut and thrust of the world of journalism.

The Guardian, unique among the press, is owned by a trust – the Scott Trust, created in 1936. It is said that the Trust is largely passive as long as everything is going right, but it appoints the editor and ensures the principles of its founders are upheld. The Guardian now has a circulation of almost 400,000 and is read by about 1.3 million readers.

William Halewood was born in Liverpool in 1840, the son of a crew-member of a sailing vessel. In his early childhood his mother used to recite and sing for her children and later he wrote 'When I asked for more she used to say make haste 'Billy'. Learn to read and then you can learn as many songs and tales as ever you want.' He took her advice and read all kinds of books, good, bad and indifferent! As he wrote down, he became 'an OMNIVEROUS READER.' There was a shop in Mill Street, Toxteth Park in Liverpool which had a large quantity of unsold numbers of Tales which had been published in penny numbers. When he had a few pence to spend, which was very seldom, he used to spend his coppers in there, as they let him have out of print copies at 3d per dozen.

William had an adventurous early life, being almost given up for dead on two occasions – he was found at the bottom of the swimming baths

when he was at school, and after becoming an apprentice at a Merseyside shipyard he, along with some others, jumped into the river, but he was sucked up by a sewage sluice and nearly drowned. About this time he became a member of the Liver-

pool Free Library and later wrote 'I mostly went there to read on a winter's night after I had left work, there being a good light there which we could not afford at my mother's cottage.'

A vicar in Liverpool suggested he leave his job at the shipyard and become an evangelist. When he was about 21 years old he went to be a lay reader at Holy Trinity Church at Tunstead in the Rossendale Valley, and was appointed to the mission school at Acre Mill. He was also elected Librarian for the Sunday School, and took the opportunity to read many of the books in it.

It was at Tunstead that he met Ann Mitchell, who was then 20 years old. Her father had died and her mother had married a widower with six children. Everyone in the area had a good word for Ann, and so he wrote, 'Naturally I came to the conclusion that such a daughter would make an excellent wife and I went about my work with renewed vigour, knowing that I had a prize in view that was well worth winning.' In 1864 he married Ann at Tunstead, and they had five children, Alfred, Bessie, Bertha, Harold and Beatrice. They had a cottage ready furnished in Mount Pleasant, on the hillside just below the vicarage, and later took a house in Main Road, which had plenty of room for William's books. It was probably at this time that he started compiling a small notebook which is a collection of his religious experience, and later he has added details of his own life.

A vicar in Preston advertised for a Scripture Reader and he got the job. He sold their furniture, auctioned his books and they moved to live in the town. Their first home was in Garden Street, for which he paid rent of £16 a year plus rates, but when he found he could not afford this, they moved to a cottage at 4s 6d a week.

William was a determined, capable young man and in 1866 he gave up his post with the church and started in business in a small shop at 153 Adelphi Street in Preston, dealing in second-hand books. At that time Preston had a population of only 20,000, but was expanding rapidly. William had only £20, which had been presented to him by the congregation at Tunstead when he left and he spent this at John Heywood's Manchester wholesale book-shop. He quickly acquired a number of patrons, among them Mr Newsham who later presented his art collection to the town, and Mr Hibbert, the architect of the Free Library. Several of these patrons cleared books from their own library shelves and gave them to William to start his business.

However, he found progress was slow and so he attended markets at Preston, Chorley,

Garstang, Fleetwood and Blackburn carrying the books on a 'Flat Top Hand Cart' to Preston market, or to the others in a couple of bags. At these markets he secured a number of regular customers. One of his early customers was a grocer named Gooch, who never could resist buying books, but he bartered for them with groceries, which William was pleased to accept! Other early customers included Anthony Hewitson, later famous for his History of the Town, and Mr Toulmin, later founder of the Lancashire Evening Post. While William was at the markets his wife minded the shop, as well as doing the housework and looking after the children.

When he went to more distant towns to acquire books he had to travel by stagecoach along poor quality roads. It was hard work, but for William it was a labour of love.

In 1867 he moved to premises in Friargate, later moving across the road to a larger shop. In the first issue of the Lancashire Evening Post on18 October 1886, there was a small advertisement for 'Temple of the Muses', 37 Friargate, Preston – that name still appears over the shop today.

William became a friend of Mr Bramwell, Preston's first librarian, and they would discuss the books which they felt were most suitable for public reading. Mr Bramwell always preferred to buy good second-hand copies for the library rather than spend the extra on new books! William saw the public library as a help to his business, because people who had borrowed books from the library would often later wish to own their own copies.

As his children grew up, they also grew to love books; his wife had given them a good example and they all worked together to make the business grow.

William's younger son, Harold, had book-shops in Christchurch, New Zealand and in

Melbourne, Australia. However, he enlisted, although over age, to serve in the First World War and was killed in action in 1918. His sister Beatrice was manageress of a branch bookshop in Preston.

When William was 82 he wrote 'I derive great pleasure in reading my notes and extracts' and later, on the same page, but at the age of 90, added 'Life in the old dog yet August 1930 WH'. His family gave him a birthday party at the Alexandra Restaurant and each one contributed either a vocal or musical item. Even at that age William still read two newspapers a day, without the aid of spectacles. Throughout his life he had been a non-smoker and total abstainer, and still took a walk through the parks each day never using a walking stick!

Alfred Halewood, William's son, born in 1871, gained a scholarship to Preston Grammar School where he had a good education. He then entered the business and carried it forward after his father's early retirement. Many fine north country libraries were sent to Friargate to be catalogued and in Alfred's time the business expanded rapidly. The Discount Book Company was opened at the Church Street/Lancaster Road bus terminal, where his sister Beatrice took charge – it was said of her that anyone entering

A page from William Halewood's diary

the shop for one book came out with two! Horace, the second son of Alfred and Jane, took over this shop after Beatrice had collapsed and died behind the counter; it sold ledgers, account books and ephemera, supplying solicitors, accountants, banks and similar bodies. Alfred regularly attended auction sales, travelling as far as Carlisle, and was well known to auctioneers and booksellers. Shortly after the First World War Alfred devoted his time to his Export Book Company, which he founded in 1919, and which had premises in Garstang Road, Preston, carrying on much trade with America.

Alfred's eldest son, Harold Rawsthorne Halewood, named after his Australian uncle, was placed in charge of a bookshop in Standishgate, Wigan, when he was 16. This included him attending sale-room and auction sales, but after two years at Wigan his father sent him to Australia to gain experience of life on a sheep farm, before taking over at 'The Temple of the Muses' – he so enjoyed his travels that he also visited New Zealand, Fiji, Tonga, and Samoa. He served with the New Zealand Division in the 1914-1918 war and was severely wounded, afterwards marrying a lady from the New Zealand hospital at Walton on Thames, where he had been treated. On demobilisation he took over the Friargate shop. He had a powerful, almost austere personality but had a common touch which endeared him to many people.

Harold and Beatrice had three children, Jean, Horace and Hilda (affectionately known as

David Halewood at No 37

Paddy) and lived over the shop. Harold's office was on the first floor and he communicated with staff in the shop through a speaking tube placed through the floor. From an early age the children helped in the shop, and when a shop assistant was indisposed they had to take turns to run both the shop and a market stall.

1942 was a memorable year for Halewood's, as on the 6th August they received an order from King George VI, from one of their catalogues. During the Second World War The Discount Book Company had an extensive trade in books on engineering and aeronautical titles – English Electric, builders of the Canberra bomber, was based in the town, and Leyland Motors were quite near by. This shop eventually closed down in 1975. During Harold's time at the helm they also owned the Preston Book Company, which sold books throughout the world by post.

Alfred was a founder member of the Antiquarian Booksellers Association, which commenced in 1906 – it is now the premier antiquarian and rare book association in the world.

During the Second World War Harold's son Horace served on the Russian convoys on HMS Norfolk with the Royal Navy. The business moved from generation to generation, and from the 1950s to the present day Horace Halewood has devoted his life to books and the business. For some years his sister Paddy also worked in the company. In 1971 Halewood's received an order, by overseas telegram, for several books from the Imperial Court, Teheran in Iran – such is their reputation. Other famous customers have included Desmond Morris, who was introduced by David Attenborough to Halewood's.

Now Horace leaves the day to day running of the two shops to his sons Michael and David, but he is still active in the business in many other ways. They specialise in Colonial History, particularly Africa and Australasia, selling to academics worldwide, but also have a vast stock on almost any subject you care to enquire about. They are no ordinary second-hand bookshop, and as their centenary booklet proclaims are truly 'Antiquarian, New and Export Booksellers since 1867'.

The Hartley family have lived in the shadow of Pendle since at least 1620. William Pickles Hartley was born in 1846, his family being grocers at Waterside in Colne, but he wanted to be a pharmacist when he left school. Unfortunately the family was not wealthy enough to let him follow his dream, and instead he joined his mother in the grocer's shop she kept. When a suitable shop became vacant in Colne main street he urged his parents to take it; they were aghast at such a proposal, but another businessman supported William's idea and he went on to develop its wholesale potential.

Regularly he walked over the wild Pennine moors to Haworth, Keighley and the nearby villages, which were so well known to the Brontë sisters. He left home at 5 o'clock in the morning and visited the first small shop-keeper by 7 o'clock, getting orders and arranging for the deliveries to be made. Some years later he recalled how often he would walk 20 miles, call on twenty customers and not make a shilling! It was a hard life, particularly in winter, and it took determination to keep going.

On the morning of Whit Monday 1866 William married Martha Horsfield. They spent their honeymoon afternoon processing round Colne with the Sunday School children, singing hymns – and the next morning returned to work! Throughout his life William was a regular worshipper and worker within the Primitive Methodist churches. In the week he worked hard

for his business, Sunday was dedicated to his Lord and His worship and service. Martha was his constant companion in their home, in church, and a wise counsellor in all his business and philanthropic affairs.

William Hartley had a dispute with a local jam manufacturer and this led him to investigate the possibility of making his own preserves.

William Hartley

Finding no suitable place in Colne he decided to move to Bootle in 1874, where he could have his own railway sidings. This location reduced the costs of transporting both fruit and sugar, and in 1886 he also built the works at Aintree. Eventually, after several extensions, the works covered ten acres. The move to the Liverpool area was against the advice of family and friends; only Martha stood by him. He sunk all his capital into the building of the new factory and had to borrow money to pay for his fruit and sugar. The loan was to run for seven years

HARTLEY'S JAM WORKS, AINTREE
A VIEW of one of the streets in Hartley's Model Village.

HARTLEY'S JAM WORKS
AINTREE

VIEW of a corner of the Kitchen where the food for employees is cooked and prepared. It adjoins the dining-hall and is on the most up-to-date lines. There are electric potato-peelers, electric dough-making machines and special steam ovens for baking. The Kitchen is equipped to supply 4,000 meals daily, and all the "washing-up" and drying is done by special machinery and appliances.

and the interest swallowed up 75 per cent of the profits; indeed he would have liked to repay the sum more quickly but those who loaned him the money refused to release him. Their early struggles were indeed severe!

W. P. HARTLEY'S Table Jellies.

ARE PURE, WHOLESOME, TRANSPARENT, DELICIOUS FLAVOUR, REASONABLE PRICE, AN ORNAMENT TO THE TABLE, RED SEAL ON THE LABEL, ONCE USED ALWAYS USED.

W P Hartley

LIVERPOOL AND LONDON.

Even during these times of great hardship, William and Martha Hartley committed in writing, on the 1st January 1877, that they would set aside a specific and well considered portion of their income for religious and philanthropic purposes, and that this would have first call on their monies before other payments were made. Later in life, as his income increased, so did the percentage of William's giving, eventually reaching 20 per cent of his gross income; never was that commitment of 1877 revoked.

In 1901 in order to better supply his increasing number of southern customers he opened premises in Southwark, London. This site covered two acres and was designed to produce over 400 tons a week, which with the 600 tons at Aintree, gave a total of 1,000 tons a week; the London factory also had storage for 5 – 6 million jam jars, all of them made of glazed stoneware. These were made in 1lb, 2lb, 3lb and 7lb sizes.

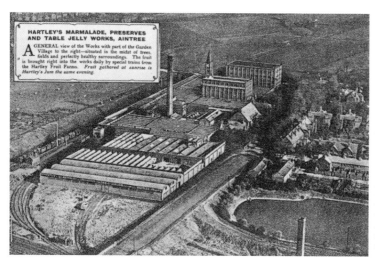

HARTLEY'S MARMALADE, PRESERVES AND TABLE JELLY WORKS, AINTREE

A GENERAL view of the Works with part of the Garden Village to the right—situated in the midst of trees, fields and perfectly healthy surroundings. The fruit is brought right into the works daily by special trains from the Hartley Fruit Farms. *Fruit gathered at sunrise is Hartley's Jam the same evening.*

In the North of England the 7lb size was kept on the counter in many shops, and from them small quantities were ladled out with a wooden spoon for poorer customers. Originally a lighthouse trademark, depicting safety, was used but this was later replaced with a pictorial label.

He had a large fruit farm in Bedfordshire and pottery works at Melling and St Helens, which supplied the containers for the jam. Generally the fruit was gathered and

preserved on the same day, and what they could not grow themselves was either grown specifically for them, or was selected carefully from the London markets. Nothing but fresh fruit and sugar were used. William tested every batch himself, often arriving at the factory at 6 o'clock in the morning and examining a thousand jars. By the beginning of the First World War his was one of the largest preserve businesses in the world. In 1919 the business was turned into a limited liability company.

In such a countryside grew the fruits for this REAL JAM

Hold on to Hartley's! This delicious real fruit jam has not altered in quality by one single berry, or by one ounce of the pure white sugar which has always gone into Hartley's jam-making. See those good deep orchard tones through the glass of the pots. That is your guarantee that Hartley's are still offering you the same goodness and real-fruit nourishment for your money.

A PROMISE

PEACE may be quick or slow in coming, but you will always be able to rely on the same HARTLEY'S for Fresh Fruit Jams at the lowest price at which jam as good as Hartley's can possibly be sold. Hartley's give you their word that they will keep QUALITY UP and PRICES DOWN as long as is humanly possible. That is our determined policy.

HARTLEY'S
The greatest name in jam-making

William Hartley also cared greatly for his workers, building a model village at Aintree – Hartley Village. It was one of the precursors of the garden village movement, ahead of Bournville and Port Sunlight. The Aintree Institute combined the purpose of a club with that of a temperance public house. Quite early on he introduced a profit sharing scheme which paid his workers a bonus, and at Aintree he paid a doctor to offer a free service to his staff. He provided both a cottage hospital and 20 cottage homes for his home town of Colne. Throughout his life he also helped many other hospitals.

Earlier mention has been made of his connection with the Primitive Methodist Church. In 1890 the Conference, its controlling body, appointed him as national Missionary Treasurer; in 1909 the Conference appointed him its President, a rare honour for a layman. On two occasions he totally covered the costs of the large extensions to their ministerial training college in Manchester, which subsequently became known as the Hartley Victoria College.

In 1908 he was knighted, becoming Sir William Hartley. He died in 1922.

Hartley's canned fruit and vegetables' range was commenced in 1933 when a pea canning section was opened at Aintree.

Hartley's was merged with Chivers in 1959 when it was bought by Chivers, then part of Cadbury Schweppes. The production facilities in London were then closed down in favour of the more modern ones at Histon.

John Whittaker was born in 1820 and in 1851 he opened a confectioner's shop in Lower Deardengate, in Haslingden. By 1866 the shop was run by John and his step-daughter, Sarah, and as business was brisk they advertised for another confectioner, subsequently offering the job to Richard Henry Holland.

Richard was born in 1848 at Cheswardine in Shropshire and became an apprentice confectioner at Bollands in Chester, before moving to Wm Moseley's Bakery at Accrington. In 1869 twenty-one year old Richard married Sarah. He had inherited £100 from his father and this he gave to Sarah, in gold sovereigns, on their wedding day. With this money they bought into John Whittaker's business, and when he retired shortly afterwards, they changed the name of the business to Holland's.

A little later they moved the business to premises in Church Street, Haslingden. Walter Holland was born there in 1870, and over a number of years they had five more children – Cissy, Ada, John, Ruth and Richard.

To enable them to enlarge the business Walter took a job with another confectioner, Fletchers in Higher Deardengate, and his wife Frances took a

Frances Isobel Holland (Walter's wife) with sons Harry and Frank in 1894

part-time job in a cycle shop. Walter's brother John worked for his father, but when Richard retired in 1890 Walter bought the business and changed its name to Walter Holland. Walter and Frances had three sons, Harry, Frank and Walter Harold (known as Harold).

In 1907 the business was transferred to the corner of Church Street and Regent Street, and the bakery was moved to larger premises in John Street. At that time Holland's were baking over 10,000 loaves a week, and Holland's pies were delivered locally by horse and cart – it was to be another twenty years before they acquired their first motor van.

The production unit was again moved in 1929 when they purchased the disused cotton mill, Industrial Mill at Baxenden, near Accrington. The renovation of these premises took several years to complete as looms were replaced with specially built ovens. Two sets of huge letters 'HOLLAND'S PIES' were purchased and were placed underneath each other down the length of the tall brick-built chimney. Local people used the chimney to help drivers who were asking for directions – telling them to 'look out for the Hollands Pie chimney'!

No sooner were the renovations completed when a new factory was built in Baxenden and they moved there in 1936. That year Walter Holland retired, leaving his

Holland's original one horse power delivery vehicle, (top), its first van, 1927 (centre) and 50s fleet (right)
Opposite: Coronation procession float outside the John St Haslingden premises, 1911. Seated front row from left are John, Frank, Walter, Richard and Harry Holland.

The dough house – where they mixed the pastry – in 1937.

sons in charge, and the firm becoming Walter Holland & Sons Ltd. They were still producing cakes, bread and fruit pies, but meat pies were the fastest growing line, with the greatest profits. By now 100,000 pies a week were being produced and the staff had increased to about 60.

By 1938 Holland's had twenty vans making regular deliveries to fish and chip shops around Lancashire. Pies cost $3^1/_2$d each, with a 6d deposit on the pudding tins. Van salesmen carried small cubes of gravy, rather like OXO cubes, wrapped in twists of greaseproof paper, which they gave to the shopkeepers. They still made cakes, such as cream horns, swiss rolls, trifles, riviera sandwich slabs, and mince tarts, but meat pies remained the favourite. With sugar rationing starting in 1939, cake production stopped.

During the Second World War, when meat was rationed, Holland's made Woolton Pies, named after Lord Woolton, the then Minister of Food. These pies were filled with carrots, potatoes, turnips and bread, as an alternative to meat – remarkably, they proved very popular and on a busy day they baked 3,500. Many of the men who worked for the company were called up, and therefore women had to take over most of the work. As petrol was also rationed, deliveries had to be restricted to within a twenty-five mile radius of the factory.

After the war, when petrol restrictions were lifted, Holland's had a request for a delivery from Jack Pye, a fish and chip shop owner in Liverpool, and gradually new rounds sprang up all over the North West – now they were supplying about 3,000 food and catering establishments.

In 1949, due to the ill health of Frank Holland, who wished to retire, and after much discussion with the other brothers, the company was sold to R Gunner Ltd, a provisions firm based in London and Liverpool for over £300,000. Harry Holland stayed on as managing director but the other two retired.

Sales rounds covered by the vans continued to increase and most of the sales were still to fish and chip shops. The salesmen were paid on a commission basis, which could present problems – O'Hagen's cafe on the Golden Mile at Blackpool sold five times as many pies in summer as they sold in winter, so the Blackpool van salesman was paid a standard wage throughout the year to prevent uneven pay packets.

In 1972 Holland's was acquired by Pork Farms. Once again it was time for a change; no longer were the pies sold in individual tins, but for the first time they were sold in foil containers. Another innovation was the introduction of automated production on both the Steak and Kidney Pie, and the Potato and Meat Pie lines.

When Northern Foods bought Pork Farms in 1979 the company became part of one of the United Kingdom's major food manufacturing groups. Within a couple of years Holland's had started to freeze pies and purchased a 40 ton refrigerated lorry so that they could distribute pies to grocery multiples throughout the North West of England.

1980 saw the completion of extensions totalling 100,000 sq ft, which, with new equipment, cost several million pounds. In 1985, following major investment in new plant such as blast freezers, and new packing and storage facilities, Holland's capacity increased significantly. Fleur de Lys of Warwick was purchased by Northern Foods in 1990 and brought into Holland's product range; production was also transferred to Baxenden. They also started supplying the catering trade with multi-portion entree dishes through cash and carry outlets and wholesale distributors. As food hygiene became of increasing importance, the company introduced specially wrapped packs for the supermarket chiller cabinets. Similarly a range of frozen ready meals, each emblazoned with the brand image and drawing attention to the value of Holland's 'special taste' traditional foods, was launched into retail outlets.

Holland's Pies were sent to Germany in 1991 to greet Lancashire Cavalry Regiment, 14th/20th Hussars when they returned from the Gulf War – they hadn't been keen on local food but relished the pies. The following year Accrington Stanley, whom Holland's sponsored, played Crewe Alexandra in the second round of the

FA cup at Ewood Park. Two of the many adverts at the time of the match read 'Accrington Stanley for the Cup – Holland's pies for the plate' and 'Easier to cut through than the Crewe defence' – sadly, Accrington Stanley lost!

After 18 months development 1993 saw the introduction of five new mouth-watering recipes – melt in the mouth shepherd's-pie, chunky beef stew and dumplings, Lancashire hot-pot, lasagne, and a fiery chilli con carne; three new frozen ready made meals also arived – beef in ale, Irish stew, and bangers and mash. By now Holland's held third place in the frozen pie and pudding market in Britain with 14 per cent – only Bird's Eye Walls (16.3 per cent) and Campbell's Freshbake (14.25 per cent) could beat them.

In 1996 Holland's introduced 'Betty's Kitchen Range' of oven ready meals, named after Coronation Street's famous cook, Betty Turpin, at the Rover's Return.

Today Holland's is the number three frozen retail brand market, with an 11 per cent share. The company not only continues to supply fish and chip shops and supermarkets, but also helps such food-service giants as Sutcliffe Catering and Gardner Merchant to satisfy their many customers.

bloggs®

Shami Ahmed

The Ahmed family came to Britain from Pakistan in 1964 and settled in Manchester. Eathasham (Shami) Ahmed was born in Karachi and was only two years old when the family made the decision that changed their lives.

When he was 15 he left school, where he had a reputation as a sharp dresser, and joined his father in setting up the wholesale clothing business, Pennywise.

His father ran Pennywise with typical Asian reserve, playing his cards close to his chest, revealing as little as possible of his plans, business decisions, or his assets. This was partly due to modesty, coming from a country where corruption in business was common.

By 1980 Manchester had already taken over from Liverpool as the music and style capital of the North and was becoming a centre for youth, fashion and street culture. The 1980s was a materialistic decade and there was money to be made out of garments. In the nine years that Shami worked with his parents, he had plenty of opportunities to get to know the market and identify a number of profitable unexplored niches in the 'rag trade'.

His first step to fame and riches came with the realisation that customers who wanted to buy jeans had a choice of either expensive

Cricketer Brian Lara

designer-label products or cheap mass-produced ones which had no pretension to fashion. Shami saw 'pre-washing' as a way of giving mass-produced jeans individual distinction, and in 1985, at the age of 24, went into business on his own account – the Legendary Joe Bloggs range of garments was born.

Joe Bloggs, based in Manchester, is Shami's own brainchild; there is also a large difference between his business style and that of previous generations of Ahmeds. In 1986 he turned back the fashion clock, re-introducing the 25" flair, whilst in 1989 he introduced the ventilation jean with metal rivets down the fly, leg and waistband! More recently Shami has sponsored Prince Naseem Hamed and introduced the 'paranormal range', linking the clothing with Uri Geller.

Shami, still only in his mid-thirties, has given Joe Bloggs an 86 per cent brand awareness, and made it a front-runner among the top ten jean manufacturers in the United Kingdom – a British brand manufactured in Britain. His whole business depends on the maximum exposure of Joe Bloggs, involving use of the media, advertising and entertainment. Top sports men and women wear his clothes and a major sponsorship deal with cricketer Brian Lara led to the Legendary Brian Lara range. Another deal brought Joe Bloggs in front of the 1991 Cup Final crowd. The Joe Bloggs name is also associated with rock music, having close links with the groups Take That, Stone Roses and Apache Indian.

The Joe Bloggs marketing philosophy is to let the world know what he is doing, and information flows from the in-house public relations department to overseas distributors in Europe, the Middle East, Malta, Russia and South Africa. Shami believes in an open style of management and employs young, dynamic staff. As part of the company's growth he has acquired the Elizabeth Emanuel brand name, a name closely associated with Princess Diana, for they made her wedding dress. The company has long since expanded to include in its range not only jeans but also toiletries, shoes and music – a complete lifestyle!

Shami may seem to be 'laid back', but as with all entrepreneurs, he is constantly on the look out for new business opportunities – using the flair and imagination that has made Joe Bloggs legendary.

KENDALS

Today we know the store as Kendals, one of the House of Fraser stores, but originally it was known as Kendal, Milne & Faulkner, silk and shawl warehousemen, general drapers – back in 1836 when the firm came into being many shops were known as warehouses.

Similarly the equivalent of the modern department store was at that time known as a bazaar. Rather like the modern shopping mall, it also boasted exhibitions, picture galleries, menageries, and other forms of entertainments as well as counters and stalls rented out to a variety of retailers.

In 1796 John Watts, who came from Didsbury, then a village near Manchester, opened a shop on the corner of Parsonage, on Deansgate in Manchester. He and his wife Betty had six sons who had been taught hand spinning and weaving. They produced woven ginghams and similar cloths. Together they made sure the shop flourished. Later they moved to rented premises, known as 'Brook's Bazaar', on the other side of Deansgate.

As far back as 1821 John Watts had placed an advertisement in the first edition of the Manchester Guardian. Ten years later he and his sons were advertising the opening of their rebuilt larger bazaar in Manchester's Deansgate. They owned the whole of the market-like building, and hired counters to merchants to sell their own wares – not unlike the modern idea of concession shops-within-shops. The Bazaar was open from 9.30am to 8pm, 9pm on Saturdays. Gradually the Watts family left the day to day work to their staff and later sold the business to three of them.

Thomas Kendal was born in 1807 in Sedbergh,

The store circa 1840 and, below, around 1900

on the edge of the Lake District. However, he soon left the rural scenes of the northern Pennines for the excitement and challenge of London, where he became a draper's assistant. The hours were long and the work difficult and demanding but he was diligent and he progressed. He worked for both retailers and wholesalers and so gained a lot of experience that would be useful to him in later life. It was while working for a wholesale firm called Fisher & Robinson that Thomas Kendal met George Moore. George had a considerable influence on Thomas and became a lifelong friend.

When Thomas was only twenty-three his health broke down through overwork and doctors advised him to rest. For a while he went back to the Lake District, but then met George Moore in Manchester, before he returned to London.

George introduced him to brothers Samuel and James Watts, and he took a position with them in 1830.

James Milne was born in Swinton in 1804 and began his working life as an apprentice in the textile trade. Adam Faulkner was born at Flixton in 1812 and he also started life working in the textile industry. They went to work for S J Watts about the same time as Thomas Kendal, and it is said that the three were like the Three Musketeers. They worked there happily for the next four years but in 1834 they were invited to buy the Bazaar, which they did. Wisely they retained the old name on the facade, but added to it the names of Kendal, Milne and Faulkner.

In 1838 Thomas Kendal lived within easy reach of the store at 47 Great Ducie Street whilst the other two partners lived on the outskirts of the city. In later years all three moved out to the more desirable areas of Cheadle, Rusholme or Prestwich and had large houses and servants. By 1842, as trade grew and capital became available they installed 'Bute Light' in the Bazaar; at that time it was the most up-to-date form of gas lighting.

By the mid-1850s after years of hard work and enterprise, Kendal, Milne and Faulkner had become accepted as one of the most reputable businesses in the area, offering quality goods and competitive prices. They had a cabinet warehouse and a delivery fleet drawn by more than fifty horses. For those living within a five mile radius of the store there were two deliveries each day. In 1862 Adam Faulkner died at the early age of fifty and as his children were only aged ten and seven, too young to join the business, the family's association with the business ceased and the company became Kendal, Milne & Co.

From old etchings we can see that the remaining partners continued to show their business acumen, for across the top of the building was the name Kendal, Milne and above the door the words 'The Bazaar'. In 1872 they demolished the old Bazaar building and rebuilt a new structure on the same site, which became known as the Main Building, whilst across the other side of Deansgate they developed the cabinetmaking side of the firm. The business continued to develop in this way; furniture and furnishings on the west side of Deansgate, men's and women's clothes and

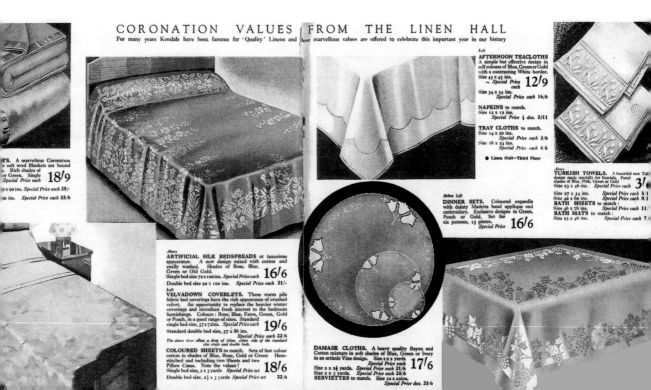

haberdashery on the eastern side, although it was in a proliferation of buildings.

In 1884, when Thomas Kendal was 77, he retired, although he still retained a lively interest in the business, and the responsibility for the store passed to John Dewhurst Milne, the eldest son of James Milne; James had died in 1866, aged 62, only four years after the death of Adam Faulkner. On Thomas' 80th birthday the employees held a special celebration in his honour and presented him with an illuminated address, subscribed to by over 600 employees. He died in 1891, aged 84, and was buried in the Heaton Mersey Congregational Burial ground. All his life he had been an active Christian man, a well loved and respected employer, and whilst not a public man, was well known for his benevolence. In conjunction with Sir James Watts he had been vice chairman of the Manchester Warehousemen and Clerks Provident Association.

John Dewhurst Milne became a Justice of the Peace, a Governor of Manchester Grammar School and of the Royal Infirmary, and Deputy Chairman of Manchester Art Gallery. He also became a partner in the business along with his younger brother James Herbert Milne, and Thomas Kendal's two sons, Samuel Kendal and Thomas Herbert Kendal.

We get a little of the essence of the business from a journalist who wrote in the Ladies Home Journal in 1892: 'Manchester has no more perfect example of a modern furnishings and textile emporium, representing nearly every department of these trades, than that afforded by the great establishment of Messrs Kendal, Milne & Co. in Deansgate. . . We have never visited an establishment in which greater care is manifested in the arrangement of the store. . . One of the foremost of English mercantile institutions. . . The flight of the lift, which takes visitors easily to the room they require, gives a breathtaking moment for an introduction to a series of the largest showrooms

ouside London.' He goes on about the elegant oriental carpets and tapestries, splendid dresses, soft raiments of artistic lines and styles. He also visited the satinwood room, specially created for the visit of the Prince and Princess of Wales in 1887, where the beautiful oriental objects reminded him 'of being in some large eastern bazaar'. He described the tea room where you could sit on comfortable divan seats, covered in terracotta coloured velvet, each nestled in alcoves on either side of the room, or 'rest in sheer luxury on saddleback chairs while sinking your feet into the softly-shaded oriental rugs'. All was enhanced with palms, ferns and oriental figures. And of course you could buy there an elegant and substantial tea!

An advertisement in 1896 highlighted the store's Mail Order Service, indicating that all parcels valued over 20s would be despatched to any railway station within the United Kingdom, 'Carriage Paid'.

In 1898 Kendal, Milne & Co. were appointed, by the Prince and Princess of Wales, as 'Upholsterers' to their royal residence; in 1901 they were appointed by the then Prince of Wales, later King Edward VII, as 'Upholsterers to the Royal Household'. Kendal, Milne & Co. also exhibited at the magnificent Irish International Exhibition in 1907.

As the family connections grew less and less, the store became vulnerable to bids from outside and in 1919 the store was taken over by Harrods for £675,000. Sir Richard Burbridge resolved in the Harrods minutes of the time that henceforth it would trade in Manchester as 'Harrods Ltd, formerly Kendal, Milne & Co.'. However, Mancunians were not impressed by the new title and exerted pressure on the Harrods board to change the name back to Kendal, Milne & Co. – within six months the board had agreed.

Further extensions continued, and in 1920 an Act of Parliament was passed allowing them to tunnel under Deansgate to provide a link between the buildings on either side of the road. The following year work not only began on the subway but a further two storeys were added to the building, adjacent to Police Street, and modern electric lifts were fitted.

The 1930s again saw much new building work. In 1936 the building on the western side of Deansgate was further extended and became known as the Centenary Building, and two years later work was started on the present building, replacing all the various structures and the old Star Hotel and its stableyard, on the Salford side of Deansgate. It was planned to carry out the work in three phases, but on the 10th February 1939 the building was gutted by fire. However, in spite of the restraints of wartime, the new building was completed.

The 1930s were also known as 'The Threadbare Thirties', the decade of unemployment, but also the days of 'The Back Britain' campaign. During those days a gramophone could be bought for 20s, shirts had detachable starched collars, and with sunbathing in vogue, new bathing costumes had backs as bare as the evening gowns of the day.

During the Second World War Kendals received a greater number of orders through the post – the Mail Order Department became very important. After years of rationing they gradually extended their services, which now included funerals and a travel agency. The 'Fashion conscious Fifties' saw the introduction of nylon and the first mass produced clothes. Later, before he signed up for BBC television, Harry Corbett, with Sooty, appeared in Kendals to the delight of younger customers.

The 1970s saw the change to decimal currency and throughout the decade the store celebrated with a series of international events, featuring Italy, United States, and Holland and also marked British achievements with transatlantic yachts-

woman Clare Francis, a Rover 3500, a midget submarine, a North Sea Oil display, and a model of Concorde.

The 70s also saw the demolition of the Centenary Building to make way for the Fraser Building and a 600 vehicle car park. The Fraser Building housed Kendals Administrative offices and the registered office of House of Fraser Midlands. A decade later it was decided to sell the furniture buildings on the east side of Deansgate and consolidate all departments in the Fraser Building.

This decision led to the redesigning and refurbishment of the building to meet the needs of the 1980s and 1990s. In the early days following this work there were personal appearances of such famous names of the eighties as 'The Saint', 'Miss  World', Jean Rook of the Daily Express, Barbara Woodhouse, and many others. There were fashion shows, talks, demonstrations, tea dances, food and wine tastings, and competitions.

Today Kendals houses eight sales floors, each with its own particular emphasis, each linked by escalators and lifts. There are ranges of the latest fashion garments and accessories, perfumes, items for the home, as well as restaurants. Thomas Kendal, James Milne and Adam Faulkner would be amazed at the present building, its computerised stock control, and its range of merchandise, but without doubt they would be pleased to see that the store they founded, probably the first true department store in the world, is still Manchester's leading 'Bazaar'.

Leyland Motors Ltd

It all began with a tricycle and an old lawn mower!

The Sumner family had long been established as blacksmiths in Leyland. In the 1861 census, Richard Sumner, his wife and young family are listed as living at 1 Water Street, which was eventually to be the birthplace of Leyland Motors.

In 1892 James Sumner, Richard's son, took over his father's engineering concern which manufactured iron and brass castings. The Lancashire Steam Motor Company was formed in 1896, but the first steam vehicle to be built and operated in Leyland dates back to 1884, when James produced a steam wagon to his own design; he intended it to carry coal from local pits to Stannings Bleachworks in Leyland, but it had only a very short life. Next James created a steam tricycle, which had a twin cylinder engine with an oil fired boiler, and upon which he and his brother William sped through the country lanes. However, such activities were unlawful, for in those days motorised vehicles had to be preceded by a man carrying a red flag.

The head gardener of a local estate presented him with an ancient lawnmower to experiment with, and using the engine from the tricycle, he made a successful machine which won first prize and a silver

SUMNER'S PATENT STEAM LAWN MOWER.

VERY STRONG
Well Made
AND
Durable.
NO DANGER.
Compact
AND
Neat.
EASY TO WORK.

Steam can be raised in ten minutes from Cold Water.

———

EASY TO START.

The Sumner patent steam lawn mower which went into production in 1893

medal at the Royal Lancashire Agricultural Show. Soon one of these machines was sold to Rugby School, and many cricket clubs and public schools also purchased them.

In 1895 James Sumner, still keen to develop a 'horseless carriage', used one of his mowing machine engines in a three wheeled car for Theodore Carr, the biscuit manufacturer of Carlisle. Although this was a great success, the company still relied on its lawn mowers as its main business.

J Sumner Ltd was formed in 1896 when T Coulthard & Co, a Preston engineering firm, took a half share in the company and J H Toulmin became a director; he eventually became chairman of Leyland Motors. Later that year George Spurrier took over the Coulthard interests and his brother, Henry Spurrier, combined his ideas with those of James Sumner. The firm now moved to a small works in Herbert Street.

The twenty men employed at the works started at 6.15am, summoned by the ringing of a huge handbell, and perhaps they picked up a draught of ale on the way, for the public houses were already open. On a Monday work started at 8am and each night finished at 5.45pm; Saturday working was until 11.45am, and all for 28 shillings a week.

The first vehicle to be produced at the new works was a 30cwt steam van which had an oil fired boiler and a two cylinder compound engine. It was taken to trials for self-propelled vehicles in Manchester and won the highest award. Their next, and larger vehicle was a three ton wagon built in 1898 which also won awards in both Birmingham and Liverpool, and perhaps even more important cash prizes of £100 on both occasions, providing useful finance for the young company, and also enabling the bosses to take their employees and their womenfolk on an outing to Windermere. The three ton wagon was bought by Fox Bros & Co of Wellington and its success suggested that coal and coke would be the boiler

The first successful vehicle

fuel of the future, rather than oil.

Their first export sale was made as early as 1901 when they shipped three Royal Mail vans to Ceylon, now Sri Lanka.

In 1902 the company bought three acres of land where they built North Works. The following year they registered the firm as a private company with a capital of £50,000, and added a further one and a half acres to the site; they now employed about 160 people. 1903 also saw the passing of the Motor Car Act, an important piece of legislation which provided for the registration of vehicles by counties, a speed limit of 20mph, and unladen weight limits. Early in the new century lawnmower production gave way to two speed wagons – the first speed gave 5-6mph and the second 6-12mph.

Their first experimental petrol engine vehicle was introduced in 1904, often called 'The Pig'; it was unpopular, reluctant to start and when it did start gave out bestial grunts! It had a two cylinder engine which produced 12bhp (brake horse power) and could carry 30cwt. It never became a production model, although some 24bhp Y types did, and these were fitted with the newly invented solid rubber tyres. Petrol engined vehicles generally travelled at higher speeds and normally had solid rubber tyres, whilst steam powered vehicles retained steel tyres.

One can imagine the joy one morning in 1905 when a contract arrived for a petrol engined double-decker for the London and Suburban Omnibus Co – the first 'Leyland' bus for London service. Repeat orders followed. Many of these were still running over 15 years later.

In 1907 Coulthards of Preston were bought out and the company changed its name from the Lancashire Steam Motor Company to Leyland

Motors Limited. Further experiments with petrol driven vehicles led to the production of the X type, which had a 35hp four cylinder engine and could carry 3.5 tons or a 34-seater bus body, and the U type which could develop 50hp. In 1910 a powerful 85hp engine was added for use on fire engines – their first fire engine was delivered to Dublin that year; thirty years later it was converted to pneumatic tyres! Other developments included the manufacture of 20-seater tramcars which were supplied to Morecambe, and also to overseas users; these weighed about 3.5 tons and could be driven from either end. The 1912 catalogue offered electric headlamps, with two sets of dynamos and also destination indicators. Progress had also been made with tyres and in 1913 the company offered a guarantee for 10,000 miles or twelve months; shock absorbers were another extra! At this time only Leyland vehicles were successful in the War Office Subsidised Vehicle Trials, resulting in the War Office ordering 88 vehicles within a twelve month period – a good order in those days. The War Office later standarised on the 3 ton model, which became known as the Leyland RAF type and fifty years later they were still working in Bombay.

The company was reconstructed in 1914 with a capital of £400,000. The organisation now employed 1,500, and up to the outbreak of war had produced 2,092 petrol engined vehicles in

A new generation changes the face of the British bus

addition to the steam wagons. The period of the First World War saw a vast amount of activity at Leyland as they fully supported the war effort, either in manufacturing new vehicles or converting others. Among the special vehicles produced were bomb carriers, radio transmitting vehicles, dentists' vans, X ray vans, mobile anti-aircraft gun platforms, and portable searchlight outfits.

After the war, branches were opened in Australia and New Zealand, with agencies throughout the East; others followed in Canada and South Africa, and proved valuable during the recession in Britain. Leyland £1 shares could be bought for 2s 3d, many orders were cancelled and prices fell – men worked four days a fortnight! The only seemingly good news was production of the Leyland straight eight cylinder car, which created a lap record at Brooklands of 117.5 mph. They also produced the Trojan car which had a 10hp 4 cylinder 2 stroke engine, which only had seven moving parts.

The production of steam wagons continued until 1926, but now the Lion range of passenger vehicles was helping rebuild the fortunes of the company. This was followed by the Titan, a six cylinder engined, low bridge type double-decker bus, which was followed in turn by the single deck Tiger. By May 1929 they had received orders for more than 1,400 Tigers and Titans. On each radi-

1918 steam lorry

ator of the T types was a badge in the shape of the head of the animal, each head hand painted in six or seven colours. At an exhibition in Manchester in 1931 they showed a chassis with a Leyland direct injection oil engine; at the same show the Leyland Cub made its debut. Efforts were also made to capture the trolleybus market, many later being supplied to the London Passenger Transport Board.

Early in 1933 a direct injection oil engine was produced – the Scottish Motor Traction group showed its confidence by ordering 250 for conversion purposes. Another feature of that year's show at Olympia was the gearless bus; smoothness and silence were its main advantages, and the following year it was the steel framed bus bodies which drew notice – advances were coming at a rapid pace.

Fire engine developments also continued and Hull received a Leyland Metz turntable escape with a 150 foot ladder in 1935, the largest ever supplied.

Much construction work took place at the Faringdon subsidiary site where a 3.5 acre engine shop was built.

Early in the Second World War it was discovered that the Leyland site featured on the Luftwaffe maps, and a new building suffered from a daylight attack. Soon the works were up and running again, now employing 11,000 workers – not only did they build vehicles but also 400,000 cast steel 1,000 lb bombs were produced each month, as well as cannon shells and even tanks.

After the War, Leyland took over West Yorkshire Foundries in Leeds. In 1946 British United Traction Ltd was formed, jointly owned by Leyland Motors Ltd and AEC Ltd. New ranges of vehicles came, including the popular underfloor engined Royal Tiger and Olympic passenger models. Soon there were other acquisitions – Albion Motors Ltd and then Scammell Lorries of Watford. A new double-decker, the MCW bodied

The Titan

78-seater Atlantean, was introduced in 1958. This rear engined vehicle with an automatic clutch and gearbox became the standard double-decker for the next twenty years. Ribble Motor Services based their 'Gay Hostess' on this model, but made it more luxurious with only 50 seats. The Leopard coach followed in 1959, and became the principal vehicle for twenty years.

1961 saw the acquisition of Standard-Triumph International which gave the company an entry into the car and light vehicle market. This was followed by its integration into Associated Commercial Vehicles Ltd, makers of AEC trucks and buses, which also included such famous names as Park Royal Vehicles Ltd, Charles H Roe Ltd, the Maudslay Motor Co Ltd and Transport Equipment (Thornycroft) Ltd. Sir Henry Spurrier retired from the position of managing director of Leyland Motors and became executive chairman of a policy forming company. The following year the Leyland Motor Corporation was formed. In 1967 they acquired the Rover Co, Rover Gas Turbines, and Alvis Ltd – Leyland now had 37.5 per cent of the UK market of heavy commercial vehicles and 10. 6 per cent of the UK car market, with a turnover of £305 million.

In 1968 it was announced that the Leyland Motor Corporation and British Motor Holdings would merge to form British Leyland Motor Corporation, the fifth largest vehicle producer in the world, the second in Europe.

At Workington, in Cumbria, work had started on a new factory for the Leyland National Co Ltd with a 1,000ft long main assembly shop for buses – it was five years ahead of the rest of the world. The 70s was a period of buoyancy for the group, but the 80s were more difficult. Within two years domestic truck sales almost halved and soon afterwards came world recession when parts of the operation had to close, with many jobs being lost. During this time Leyland Motors was re-ordered to form Leyland Truck and Bus, prior to it being merged with DAF Trucks in 1987 under the Government privatisation programme.

The recession in 1992 brought many difficulties both in Britain and Holland, and in 1993 a successful management buyout reformed Leyland Trucks, it becoming once again an independent British truck manufacturer. The company is now part of the American PACCAR Organisation, the world's second largest truck manufacturer, and today Leyland Trucks staff are designing trucks not only for the British market but also ones to be built in the United States for their market.

1956 Tiger cub

Fred Jones was a salesman, and Charles Allan a chemist at Crown Paints in Darwen in the early 1920s. Although oil matt paints were available they were expensive, and as a cheaper alternative many homes were decorated with distemper, which was made from a combination of coloured chalk, water and glue – its main disadvantage was that it could not be washed. A new emulsion paint was developed which fell between these two, and was given the famous name of 'Walpamur'.

Fred and Allan struck a deal with Crown at the birth of the product which became very remunerative; indeed Crown could not afford to retain them. The two men therefore left Crown, taking with them their formula and set up their business in Leyland in 1922, as the 'Leyland Paint and Varnish Co Ltd'. They chose Leyland as it was on good traffic routes, and mid-way between London and Glasgow; now they called their product 'Leytex'. These early emulsion paints 'Walmpamur' and 'Leytex' incorporated linseed oil to make oil bound water paints, which were more washable than the distemper. Today's 'emulsion paints' are a mixture of water and plastic resin, either vinyl or acrylic, and these are truly washable and can be used indoors or externally.

The firm built a purpose built factory, laboratory and showroom in Leyland, and also had a showroom in Oxford Street, London. Unusual among paint manufacturers, they made their own resins for use in their gloss paints and became renowned for the quality of their paint, using the slogan 'The Paint the Painters Use', which proved to be a first class phrase. The company's logo was designed by a Leyland artist, the same one who designed the Leyland Motors logo. During the years of the Second World War the company supplied large quantities of paint to Leyland Motors, for the painting of tanks and trucks.

By 1937 the Leyland Paint Company had fifteen branches nationwide from Glasgow to Bournemouth, from Sheffield to Belfast. Even after the difficult early post-war period the number of branches had risen to 33.

Additional factories were built in Kenya and South Africa, the latter having branches in Capetown, Port Elizabeth and Johannesburg. By now the company was exporting its products all over the world, and in the sixties it went public.

Later in the 1960s they diversified into wallpaper production and acquired, and developed, the Paragon Wallpaper Company in Darwen. With both paint and wallpaper to sell, the company needed a large chain of high street shops to complement its trade branches. Leyland merged with John Matthew, a Liverpool based retail paint company, who produced the first non-drip

Wallpaper printing machine, 1960

gloss paint 'Jellipex' and this helped their retail aspirations.

Unfortunately, as with several other paint manufacturing companies who became involved in making wallpapers, Leyland Paint Company ran into financial difficulties in the 1970s and early 1980s; the oil crisis of the period compounded their difficulties. Darwen traditionally had been the centre of this industry, as the machinery used for printing cottons was also suitable for printing wallpapers. However, in the years that followed, new high speed, high quality machines, which could also print vinyls, became available. These were costly to purchase and install, and unfortunately at the same time that they were being brought into use, the market for wallpapers started to decline, resulting in a number of companies running into financial difficulties.

The company, now called the 'Leyland Paint & Wallpaper Co Ltd' poured large resources into the ailing wall-covering side of the firm but ignored the profitable and relatively trouble free paint business. Finally, in deep financial crisis, profitable parts were sold off, shops were sold, and the wall-covering business also went; many employees were made redundant.

Leyland Paints was already a limited company, and Kalon, a smaller privately owned retail paint company based in Yorkshire, arranged a reverse takeover in the mid 1980s which enabled them 'to go public'. Production of the 'Leyland' brand was switched to Birstall, near Wakefield. Leslie Silver had formed the Silver Paint and Lacquer Co. (SPL), which became Kalon. It was a fast growing company and later acquired Novodec in France in the early 1990s and a few years later merged with Euridep, a subsidiary of Total, the petrol company.

In 1999, Total and Petro Fina oil companies merged and subsequently Kalon have merged with Sigma Paints (Petro Fina's paints' business) to become SigmaKalon. Kalon were delisted from the London Stock Exchange and are now a wholly-owned subsidiary of Total Fina.

Today SigmaKalon have increased the production of Leyland paints to more than five times that of the founding company and their annual turnover now exceeds £1 billion a year.

Manchester Airport

The first purpose-built airfield in Manchester was situated alongside Ashburton Road, at Trafford Park. The first landing there took place on 7 July 1911, but Louis Paulhan had landed his

aviation use, thus preventing the city having the first municipal owned airport in the country, and all flying ceased at Alexandra Park later that year.

By 1926 pressure was growing for Manchester to have its own airport links with the world. One of those pressing for this was John Leeming, chairman of the Lancashire Aero Club, a friend of Sir Sefton Brancker, the Director of Civil

biplane in a field at Burnage a year earlier to claim the Daily Mail prize of £10,000 as the first man to fly from London to Manchester.

In 1918 the War Department opened a major airfield at Hough End Fields, later named Alexandra Park, after the nearest railway station.

The first ever transport flight to Manchester was made by a Handley Page 0/400 bomber, operated by Handley Page Ltd, which landed on 1 May 1919, carrying eleven passengers from Cricklewood, in North London. The flight took three hours forty minutes and was piloted by Lt Col Sholto Douglas, who became chairman of BEA. Twenty-five days later the first scheduled domestic air service in Britain began when the Avro Transport Company operated Avro 504Ks between Alexandra Park, Southport (Birkdale Sands) and Blackpool (South Shore) – the service ran for just 18 weeks.

Daimler Airways started the first international service from Manchester with a regular schedule to Amsterdam via Croydon in 1922, but this ceased early in 1924. Lord Egerton refused to sell his land to the City Council for continuing

Louis Paulhan lands his biplane at Burnage in 1910

Aviation. In September 1928, following a series of meetings between Manchester Corporation and the Chamber of Commerce, a special sub-committee of the Corporation was formed to see whether it was possible to develop an airport in the area. The committee moved quickly and on 31 October chose Barton as the best site. On 9 November the Council set up an Aerodrome Special Committee which was charged with 'enquiring and reporting upon the establishment and maintenance of the Aerodrome at Chat Moss and the financial aspect thereof'. The committee clerk was Sam Hill, who had joined the Town Clerk's Department in 1902, and he subsequently became the first airport manager.

On 2 April 1929 Wythenshawe aerodrome opened as a temporary site while Barton was being prepared. On 22 April the Lord Mayor of Manchester, Col George Westcott, and his party flew from Manchester to Croydon to collect Aerodrome Licence No 1414, valid for an initial six months. Other interesting facts connected with this site include its use by a Gypsy Moth of Air Taxis, which was later used by Amy Johnson to make her first female solo flight from the United Kingdom to Australia in 1930.

From the beginning Manchester airport had its own customs facilities. Chat Moss had an all grass landing area of 530 yards by 670 to 740 yards, depending on the arrival point – it was never large enough for the more advanced airliners, but a large hangar and control tower were also built there.

Barton Airport opened on 1 January 1930 with Northern Air Lines making the first recorded landing on 4 January; they became its first managers and a major user. The first scheduled service was a thrice weekly one operated by Imperial Airways on a Croydon-Birmingham-Manchester-Liverpool route. The first round trip was flown on 17 June 1930, using a 20 seat Argosy 1, but the service closed down for the winter on 20 September. It wasn't until May 1933 that a wireless and meteorological station opened at Barton, operated by the Air Ministry, but with support from Manchester Corporation. Initially KLM would not use the site until the runways were extended, and due to several difficulties with the site the Corporation reviewed its options and decided to build a new airport at Ringway – at the vast cost of £179,295 for the 'initial scheme', plus a further outlay of £45,160 should air traffic developments warrant it. The recommendation was accepted by 55 votes to 54! The site had many advantages, not least that grass runways up

The airport's first pressurised airliner, 1949 (top) and, below, a New York bound Boeing 707, early sixties.

Barton in 1948 and, overleaf, aerial view of Ringway airport, 1997

to 2,000 yards long could be laid out when required.

Sir Kingsley Wood, the Air Minister, performed the official opening on 25 June 1938. The previous day a KLM Douglas DC2-PH-AKP 'Perkoetoet' arrived from Amsterdam with an official party. Airline operations began that same week, initially without navigational aids – these were not added until early in 1939; winter usage was extremely limited. Passengers in the fourteen months up to August 1939 had totalled 7,600, but all civilian services stopped on 1 September due to the outbreak of the Second World War.

During the War Ringway was more a centre for aircraft production than an air base. Two hangars were built, primarily for the use of 613 Squadron and the RAFVR, and these were followed by a further ten. When more intensive flying by heavy aircraft took place there were problems with the grass landing strips and in 1941 the Air Ministry started to construct tarmac runways and hard pans on which the aircraft could stand. Ringway was also used for the training of staff at the 'Central Landing School' in the use of both parachutes and gliders. Its proudest war-time achievement was the training of 60,000 Allied paratroopers. At its peak, in 1943, over 1,500 men and women, from both the RAF and Army, lived in prefabricated buildings or requisitioned council houses in the area.

Scheduled services finally resumed in June 1946, when a Dakota of Air France arrived from Le Bourget Aiport, Paris. Early operators included Scottish Airlines, Isle of Man Air Services, Skyways, Compagnie Air Transport and Railway Air Services. Some charter flights used the airport.

British European Airways came into being on 1 February 1947, taking over the services of almost all the United Kingdom internal airlines. KLM and Aer Lingus also introduced new schedules that year, giving regular connections to Amsterdam and Dublin, and John Mahieu Aviation gave links with Brussels.

The first civilian helicopter to visit Ringway was a Westland Sikorsky 5. 51 demonstrator in September 1947, whilst the first large four engined passenger aircraft, a Transocean Airlines Douglas Skymaster, was diverted to Ringway from Burtonwood. Another milestone was the arrival of a 245 Squadron Gloster Meteor F.4 jet in 1948 – the first ever visit of a jet aircraft. However, the rising number of passengers meant that the original 1938 terminal was unable to cope and the former parachute training school buildings were converted to create extra room. In 1949 KLM introduced the Convair 240 on the Amsterdam-Ringway-Dublin service – it was the

first pressurised aircraft to serve Manchester. An important flight that year was the departure of the Halle Orchestra en route for Amsterdam – two DC4s and two DC3s were needed to carry them and their instruments!

The continuing problem of ownership was again raised in 1950 at a meeting between Lord Pakenham and the Airport Committee, and it was agreed that it would remain in the Corporation's hands, with the Ministry providing funds for development, but the problem wasn't finally resolved until a few years later. As a result of this decision, work started on extending Runway 06-24 to a length of 5,900 feet, and installing ground controlled approach radar equipment. On 1 April 1952 round the clock operations commenced at the airport and that year it handled 163,000 passengers!

Coronation year saw the first appearance of the Viscount 701 turbo-propeller powered airliner. It was the same year that Manchester became truly international when a Douglas DC-6B left Ringway for New York, refuelling at Gander – the flight time to Gander was 10 hours 22 minutes, against strong head winds; the return, non-stop flight, took 11 hours 20 minutes. By 1954 passenger levels had risen to 265,000 for the year, three times those of 1949. BOAC was among other airlines to increase services, theirs being flights from

London-Manchester-Prestwick-New York using Boeing Stratocruisers. That year the name Ringway was dropped in favour of 'Manchester Airport',

and the one millionth postwar passenger left, for the Isle of Man.

Once again plans were put in hand to extend the facilities as the Committee projected further huge growth by 1963 – they foresaw passenger figures doubling to 525,000; in actual fact they reached 1,205,000! Manchester Airport saw the first inclusive tour service to Ostend. Such services were mainly responsibles for the vast increase in traffic in future years.

In 1958 Manchester welcomed its first jet airliner – an Air France Caravelle but Sabena introduced the first scheduled jet service with a Boeing 707 on 20 April, 1960 to New York. BOAC introduced their Rolls Royce powered Boeing 707s that same October on the flight from Manchester via Prestwick to New York.

In 1962 the Duke of Edinburgh opened the new terminal, now Terminal 1 – the domestic pier could handle nine aircraft and the international one eleven aircraft; there was also car parking facilities for 1,300 cars. The next year BOAC introduced flights starting from Manchester via Prestwick to New York. Other new aircraft of this period included the BAC One-eleven, Boeing 727, Trident 1s and VC10s. Throughout this period the main runway was lengthened several times, reaching 9,000 feet by 1968. That year a new record was set when a Caledonian Boeing 707 made the longest non-stop jet flight from Manchester, covering the 3,450 miles to Toronto, with 188 passengers and eleven crew, in 6 hours 55 minutes. It was also the heaviest take-off at 131. 25 tons, using a runway only 7,900 feet in length! In 1970 the first Boeing 'Jumbo 747' arrived.

Following Local Government reorganisation in 1974, management of the airport was vested in the Manchester Airport Joint Committee, representing the joint equal interests of Manchester City Council and the newly created Greater Manchester County Council. In 1975 the airport was renamed 'Manchester International Airport' and in 1976 was visited by its first Concorde, which had been diverted on a flight between Washington and Heathrow! In 1978, following the publication of the Government's White Paper, Manchester was nominated as the only Category A airport outside London in England and Wales – it was now 'officially' a major airport!

Freddie Laker became an important name at Manchester, carrying passengers on cheap flights to Miami and other resorts, but in 1982 his venture came to an unfortunate end when his aircraft were impounded in lieu of outstanding charges.

With the impending abolition of the Greater Manchester County Council in 1986, it was agreed that a public limited company, Manchester Airport plc be formed to ensure the continuing local ownership of the enterprise – in its first full year of operation it made a profit of £20 million. 1987 saw a pleasing development when for the first time for many years a Manchester based airline, Air 2000, flew an aircraft in direct from Seattle.

During the past decade there have been further tremendous initiatives. In 1993 the airport opened its own railway station – and Terminal 2, which doubled the Airport's terminal capacity to around 20 million passengers a year; the cost was £265 million. Phase 2 of this development is due to be completed in 2005. In 1995 a new British Airways maintenance hangar was completed at a cost of £27 million and in 1997 approval was given for a second runway. Manchester is now the world's 18th largest airport in terms of international passengers and each year over 17 million passengers and 100,000 tonnes of freight and mail pass through it to all parts of the world.

MANCHESTER
SHIP CANAL

Two hundred and fifty years ago travelling around in Lancashire was very difficult — roads were no more than muddy rutted tracks, and yet the textile industry was starting to develop. Taking finished goods to Liverpool, for shipping to the world's markets, was hazardous and expensive. The initial stage was to get the goods to Warrington, from where they were transferred from the horse drawn wagons to packhorses or on to barges which passed along the various rivers. The developing mill towns also needed raw materials and food for their workers, and suppliers had the same problems of transport as the merchants.

Improving communications between Manchester and Liverpool was first mooted in 1697 in letters between a Mr Morris and a Mr Patten; the latter was responsible for making the Mersey navigable as far as Warrington. In 1714 a group of men, called 'the undertakers' formed a company and applied for an Act 'for making the rivers Mersey and Irwell navigable from Liverpool to Manchester'. It wasn't until 1720 that the Act was passed; the same year that the first Liverpool Dock Act was passed, a very significant decision for the future of Manchester people. However, the Mersey and Irwell Navigation project, due to difficulties in controlling water levels, had to eventually withdraw and leave the future to the Bridgewater Canal, and the Manchester Ship Canal.

Daniel Adamson

In 1761, when the first and second sections of the Bridgewater Canal were opened, the Duke of Bridgewater proved that he could transport coal from his collieries at Worsley, into the heart of Manchester, for half the cost of using packhorses. Indeed it was the subsequent drop in the price of coal which led to the increased prosperity of the area. Later the Duke extended his canal, firstly to Runcorn town, and then via a flight of locks to the Mersey at Runcorn in 1773. However, due to the limited depth of water, it could only take barges of

Queen Victoria opens the canal in 1894

up to fifty tons.

Early in the nineteenth century the Bridgewater Canal was linked to the Leeds and Liverpool at Leigh, and in 1830 the Manchester – Liverpool railway was also opened. In a hundred years communications had improved greatly, but Manchester still had its problems. Liverpool Dock Board imposed extremely high dues on all goods passing through the port, an area defined as stretching from the Dee to Warrington. This meant that traders paying such fees priced themselves out of the market and many inland companies went out of business. It cost less to bring corn from America to Liverpool than to transport it from Liverpool to Manchester. Manchester became a dying city!

In 1824 Matthew Hedley, a Manchester grocer, became an advocate for a ship canal, and the following year a company was formed to move the project forward. The proposal was for a canal which would accommodate vessels capable of bearing 400 tonnes burden and upwards which would move directly between Manchester and the Irish Sea. This failed to get parliamentary approval in 1825, and it wasn't until 1885 that the necessary Bill was finally passed.

Whilst these procedures were being fulfilled, Sir John Rennie made a complete survey of the River Mersey between Bank Quay and Runcorn to assess the possibility of making the river navigable for the proposed vessels; similarly H R Palmer FRS and John F Bateman were asked to prepare alternative reports for the improvement of the River Irwell. Another significant initiative was the writing of a letter to the Manchester Guardian by a Scotsman, George Hicks, in 1876, who expressed his concern at the neglect of the River Irwell and raised the question as to why it could not be converted into a ship canal. A London engineer, C E Fulton, wrote to Hicks saying he had just completed the restoration of the Nene navigation, a waterway from the Wash to London by way of the Grand Union Canal, and that he would be very pleased to deal with the Mersey and Irwell. Subsequently he presented a report, although for the time being nothing actually happened, it shattered complacency in Liverpool, and the rail and port companies made drastic cuts in their rates.

In 1881 public interest in the proposed canal was revived following news of work done in Glasgow where 'they had brought the sea to their doors'; Newcastle-upon-Tyne had also widened and deepened the entrance to the Tyne and the Suez Canal had been opened.

It was Daniel Adamson who was the man of vision, the one who was to inspire others and drive the project forward. An engineer with a boiler-making business in Dukinfield, he was a deeply religious man who did what he thought was right with conviction and fervour. Earlier he had been engineering manager of the Stockton and Darlington Railway, and between 1887-89 was President of the Iron and Steel Institute, being awarded their Bessemer Gold Medal in 1888.

On 27 June 1882 Daniel Adamson called a meeting at his home, The Towers, Didsbury, to which he invited the Mayor of Manchester and those of surrounding towns, commercial leaders, representatives of the co-operative and labour movements and several well known capitalists. He also invited C E Fulton, and Leader Williams, who had been engineer to the Bridgewater Navigation Company. At the end of the meeting three resolutions were passed supporting the construction of a tidal canal. Two plans were then developed, one by C E Fulton, the other by Leader Williams. It was the latter one which was accepted, this being for a canal with several levels maintained by locks, as there is a 60 foot rise from the Mersey estuary to Manchester.

In July 1882, on the motion of Councillor Bosdin Leech, later Sir Bosdin Leech, Manchester Corporation resolved 'to take up the question of the canal with the vigour and earnestness which its importance demanded'. The resolution caused consternation in Liverpool, and the Manchester press were critical, believing the enterprise to be beyond the orbit of the corporation. Towards the end of the year many Manchester aldermen and councillors contributed to a £25,000 guarantee fund, but nothing was contributed from the coun-

cil's coffers. However, later the equivalent of a twopenny rate, £18,000, was agreed by Manchester Corporation, and Warrington contributed £2,000 and Salford £6,000 towards parliamentary expenses.

When news of the final parliamentary approval was relayed to Manchester, church bells were rung, cannons were fired, and bands paraded in the streets. Daniel Adamson's carriage was met by workmen who took the horses from their shafts and themselves dragged the carriage to his home, such was the rejoicing! Saturday 3 October 1885 was declared a public holiday in Manchester. It was necessary to raise £8 million before construction work could start, and as it was a Lancashire project, Adamson felt that it should be financed locally. Shares were fixed at £10 each, but this was more than Manchester working class people could afford. Adamson asked his 700 workers if they would contribute to the project. His great-grandson, Roderick Parkyn, relates: "In those days they paid one penny per day for hot water for their tea. In addition they all agreed to pay an extra penny per day towards the Ship Canal funds. And it was always said that what with tea-water and sea-water there were nowt in pay packet!"

Unfortunately the response to this scheme was disappointing and it was withdrawn; again there was disappointment when Rothschilds were unable to raise the necessary capital. The existing board was replaced by people who could meet this need. Initially Adamson stayed on as chairman but eventually retired, still expressing his confidence in the project and wishing it every success. On 4th July 1887 the property of the Bridgewater Navigation Company, which included the rights of the Mersey and Irwell Navigation Company, was purchased, by cheque, for £1,710,000 – the largest cheque ever drawn up to that time!

On the 15th July Baring Brothers and Rothschild & Sons issued a new prospectus, the Board of Trade issued a certificate confirming that statutory requirements had been met, lands were purchased, and the contract was let to T A Walker who had built the Severn Tunnel.

The work was divided into nine sections, and huts and other accommodation were provided to house the 16,000 workers. It would take these men six years to complete their task; they were paid $4^1/_2$d per hour. They had to remove from the dry excavations over 53 million cubic yards of material, 12 million being sandstone much of which had to be dredged; the workers moved between one and two million cubic yards a month!

T A Walker, the contractor, died in 1889, and amid much controversy the canal company had to take over the contract. On top of this there were many other problems with the work, and a financial crisis was averted only with the help of Manchester Corporation.

The canal, the 'Big Ditch' as it was affectionately called, was opened along its full length on 1 January 1894 amid great rejoicing. On that day an armada of ships headed by a graceful steam yacht 'The Norseman' with the directors of the company on board, made passage of the 36-mile long waterway through to the terminal docks, with many thousands thronging the banks to view the spectacle. In May 1894 Queen Victoria, on board her yacht SS Enchantress, performed the opening ceremony.

As more and more trade was handled by the canal, the country's first purpose-built industrial estate was built, Trafford Park. In addition a dock was formed on part of the old Manchester racecourse and this was opened by King Edward VII in 1905. In 1954 Queen Elizabeth Dock was opened; it was developed specifically to handle petroleum products, chemicals and bulk edible oils.

Today the Manchester Ship Canal, still one of the world's greatest industrial, commercial and transportation developments, is part of Peel Holdings plc. It changed the fortunes of Manchester for all time.

Mersey Tunnels

Although people have always crossed the Mersey by boat, just over a hundred years ago it was agreed that other means were needed. A railway tunnel under the Mersey was opened in 1885, but it was nearly fifty years before a road system under the Mersey came into being.

Goods ferries brought horse drawn and early motor traffic to and from the city, but as the economic development of Liverpool, Birkenhead, and the more distant parts of Cheshire and North Wales took place, this proved inadequate. Various suggestions were put forward by the Cross-river Traffic Committee when it was established in 1912, including having a bridge over the river, but it wasn't until 1922 that a positive decision was made. That year Sir Archibald Salvidge tabled a motion in Liverpool City Council that a committee of six be appointed to enquire and report on the possibility of a scheme of Merseyside federation, and the improvement of transport facilities including the provision of a Mersey bridge or tunnel. This motion was passed and Liverpool City Council invited the Boroughs of Birkenhead, Wallasey and Bootle to each nominate six representatives to meet with those from Liverpool. Sir Archibald Salvidge was appointed chair-

The Birkenhead tunnel under construction

man and they commissioned Sir Maurice Fitzmaurice and Sir Basil Mott to consult with John A Brodie, Liverpool's City Engineer, on the merits of either a bridge or a tunnel.

After about twelve months they came out strongly in favour of driving a tunnel; they pointed out that a bridge would cost about £10.5 million, have high long-term maintenance costs, in the event of war a bridge would be vulnerable to attack, and if damaged, the Port of Liverpool would become inaccessible. On the other hand a double-deck tunnel was estimated to cost £6.4 million, was not so vulnerable and would have lower running costs. The second option was therefore accepted.

The initial idea was that four lanes of traffic would be accommodated on an upper level, whilst underneath two lanes of tramcars would run on the floor of the tunnel. However, this proposal was later dropped and in the end only Liverpool and Birkenhead authorities took responsibility for the building of the Mersey Tunnel. Government help in funding the tunnel was sought, but until January 1925, when Winston Churchill, then at the Treasury, announced a capital contribution of £2.5 million with permission to charge tolls for twenty years, the offers had been too low. However, on this basis the committee resolved to go ahead, but parliamentary powers were still needed; in August 1925 the Mersey Tunnel Bill was given Royal Assent. This called for the setting up of a statutory authority, the Mersey Tunnel Joint Committee. Subsequent Bills acknowledged a cost of £7.7 million, and it was agreed that to help meet this, tolls could be charged for a total of 40 years.

To enable the work to proceed a number of buildings had to be demolished in both Liverpool and Birkenhead, especially near the entrances to the tunnels. Thought also had to be given as to where to dispose of the vast amounts of rock which would be excavated from below the river

bed; on the Liverpool side it was used to help create the Otterspool Promenade, and on land reclamation in the Dingle area, nearer to Pier Head and on the Birkenhead side it 'filled in' Storeton Quarry.

The initial work consisted of sinking two vertical shafts, each 200 feet deep, one at George's Dock (named after George III) in Liverpool, the other at Morpeth Dock in Birkenhead. On 16 December 1925 H R H Princess Royal (Princess Mary Viscountess Lascelles) switched on the power for the electric drills at George's Dock, and on 10 March 1926 Sir Archibald Salvidge, using a pick and shovel, commenced the Birkenhead excavation. Engineers then drove two pilot headings,

Sir Archibald Salvidge breaks through

an upper and a lower one, simultaneously from each bank of the river, to meet under mid-river; the lower heading was kept 150 feet in advance of the upper one. One hundred feet boreholes were drilled riverwards from the working face and once it had been established that everything was satisfactory, a battery of compressed air drills was used, followed by gelignite. Much of this work was complicated, it being necessary to explore the rock strata in advance of larger excavations taking place. Work continued twenty-four hours a day, six days a week.

On 3 April 1928, twenty-seven months after the start of the work, Sir Archibald Salvidge, in the presence of the Lord Mayor of Liverpool, broke down the thin wall of rock that separated the two sides on the lower heading – on the other side was the Mayor of Birkenhead with the Birkenhead members of the Joint Committee. The divergence of the two tunnels was about only one inch, a remarkable piece of engineering!

It was decided that the upper part of the main tunnel should be excavated to its full dimension of 46 feet 3 inches, and be lined before the rock in the lower half was removed. Much of the work was carried out by Irish navvies; at times there were up to 1,700 men working on the tunnel. Many wore metal plates on the their left boot (the one with which they usually pushed down the spade) and they could be heard clanging down the cobbled roads as they walked to their lodgings – many of the navvies were Catholics, and later Catholics in that area became known as 'left-footers'!

The excavation was so accurate that the cavity between the lining and the rock face averaged less than six inches; this was filled with small pieces of rock over which a cement grouting was pumped which cemented the lining to the bedrock. The cast-iron plates or segments which line the tunnel, made by the Stanton Ironworks at Ilkeston, weighed 82,000 tons and are held together by a million bolts. All the electrical control gear was supplied by Metropolitan Vickers, and reduction gearing, which had lead gaskets, was supplied by David Brown of Huddersfield.

The roadway was built of reinforced concrete across the main tunnel 18 inches below the horizontal diameter – this gave a maximum width consistent with roof clearance for vehicles. The roadway was surfaced with diamond studded cast iron setts, laid on a bituminous bed on the reinforced concrete. However, the surface of the setts became polished and asphalt was laid over them.

On either side of the roadway was a two foot wide raised paved footwalk, under which the various services were laid, and from which emergency exits could be accessed; these lead to a series of staircases up to ground level. Finally the tunnel walls were rendered and spray painted.

The tunnel was opened in 1934 by King George V and named 'Queensway' in honour of his wife, Queen Mary. The royal and distinguished guests had no idea that at the crucial moment the electric mechanism for lifting the curtain failed and was cranked up by hand by two unseen men! Prior to the opening the general public had been allowed to walk through the tunnel for charity.

In such a large tunnel, with vehicles continually pumping out carbon monoxide fumes, adequate

The 'mole' bores out the Wallasey Tunnel

and efficient ventilation was crucial and six ventilating stations were built. These house 28 foot
diameter fans in the exhaust units and slightly
smaller fans in the blower units. The reinforced
concrete air ducts are the full height of the buildings, and the ventilating machinery is designed to
cater for widely varying traffic densities, and
resultant changing atmospheric conditions.

The George's Dock building at Pier Head,
Liverpool, houses the administrative offices of the
organisation, and also the control room of the
Mersey Tunnel. Instruments continually measure
visibility and carbon monoxide levels in the tunnel, check traffic flows, and watch for incidents or
fires. At each entrance vehicle counters record
numbers of vehicles entering and leaving the tunnels; weight restrictions do exist and vehicle
weights can be measured at the weighbridge at
Kingsway Tunnel.

In wet weather quite an amount of water
enters the tunnel due to the downward gradient,
and water drains off the vehicles passing through;
other water is present as groundwater in the sandstone due to the rising water table of the area. All
the water is collected in a comprehensive drainage

system and returned to the River Mersey.

In 1958, with traffic flows of 10 million a year,
and growing rapidly, it was decided to build a second tunnel linking Wallasey to Liverpool. This
time, instead of building one large tunnel, with
four traffic lanes, it was proposed to build two
separate tunnels, each with two lanes; this
required the excavation of much less material,
and with the use of a mechanical mole the work
was completed speedily. This new tunnel was
named 'Kingsway' by Queen Elizabeth II in honour of her father, when she opened it in 1971.

The initial forty year period during which tolls
could be collected has been extended to cover running costs and debt charges. The collection of
tolls has now been automated and many regular
users use Fast Tag, prepayment units.

Although normally there are two lanes of traffic flowing in each direction in Queensway and
Kingsway it is possible at peak times to operate
'tidal flows'; in the morning rush hour there can
be three lanes of traffic taking workers towards
Liverpool, and only one lane takes people away
from the city.

The Mersey Tunnel Traffic Police control
observance of the tunnel's bye-laws, oversee the
flow of traffic using a comprehensive closed circuit television system, and there is a rapid
removal service for any vehicle which breaks
down in the tunnel. Certain loads can only pass
through the tunnel under police escort, and others such as petroleum products and explosives are
completely banned. Both tunnels operate 24
hours a day 365 days a year; and continuous engineering cover ensures smooth and safe operation.

Today Mersey Tunnels is a department of
Merseytravel, the trading name for the
Merseyside Passenger Transport Authority, a
local authority with elected representation from
Liverpool, Wirral, Sefton, Knowsley and St
Helens District Councils. The two tunnels carry a
total of 26 million vehicles a year.

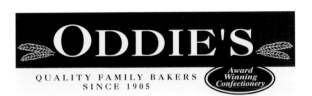

QUALITY FAMILY BAKERS
SINCE 1905

Award Winning Confectionery

In each county there are many companies who are well known in their own locality as a company of great excellence, but are perhaps not known throughout the rest of the county. Oddie's Bakery is one of these and yet they won national fame by gaining the title 'British Bakers of the Year 1993'.

It all started in a shop at 21 Primet Bridge, Colne where the bakehouse was in the cellar, under the shop. William Henry Oddie married Jane Dean in April 1908 and these were the premises where they made their first home and started their business.

William had served an apprenticeship as a baker and confectioner with George Porter in Accrington, but on returning to Colne joined his two elder sisters in a small business in the town's Albert Road before going to Primet Bridge.

In about 1914 he opened a second shop at 323 Leeds Road, Nelson, also acquiring the next door premises where he transferred the bakehouse from Colne. Ona Hodgkinson joined the business when she was fourteen years old and stayed with them for over fifty years. William Oddie had two younger sisters, Bertha and Beatrice, both of whom joined the business.

In those early days they did not have any vehicles of their own, and used a carrier to take the goods to the Colne shop, on a horse-drawn flat-cart.

John (Jack) Dean Oddie, their only child, was born in 1912 at Primet Bridge. Expansion came slowly – a third shop was opened in 1919 at 29 Scotland Road, Nelson and at the same time premises were rented in Colbran Street, previously used by a firm of dry-salters, where he produced bread and tea cakes, confectionery still being produced at the Leeds Road premises. Also about this period William acquired two vans, along with two horses to draw them.

The firm also invested in some simple mechanisation – a Gillespie Divider and Hander Up – a machine which divides the dough into pieces and delivers them on for 'proving', but it wasn't very gentle with the dough and it was not a success. One of their early employees at Primet Bridge, Harold William Bass, later came back to the company and took charge of decorating all their celebration cakes

William Henry Oddie and Jane with son John Dean and Jane's parents and brother

as well as developing many of the cream and confectionery lines the company still makes today.

In the 1920s William Oddie acquired the business of Ogden & Son (Bakers, Confectioners and Caterers) at 129 Scotland Road, Nelson, where the bakery is today, but had to borrow a lot of money during a period of high inflation – consequently the investment took many years to pay for itself. The premises consisted of a bakery shop, living quarters where William and his family lived until 1929, a bakery, and a large ballroom which could accommodate over a hundred people for dances and weddings – it was known as the

Oddie's Assembly Rooms. Previously Oddies had done a lot of outside catering and now the two were amalgamated, and were a prominent part of the firm's activities until the 1950s – the present office accommodation was the family home! Now was the time to move bread and tea cake production to 129 Scotland Road and all the confectionery production to Colbran Street. For a period the firm also became wholesale bakers, supplying other shops in the neighbourhood.

The years of the Depression had a devastating effect on the area, and the Lancashire cotton industry was badly hit. As with all firms Oddie's turnover dropped dramatically and in some years it was necessary to reduce wages to maintain a viable business. However, William refused to use inferior materials, which would have probably given him a better profit, a policy still followed today.

In 1926 the firm made its first venture into trading in nearby Burnley, taking premises in the town centre at 38 St James Street, premises still owned by Oddie's, 71 years later. Instead of buying a new van at that time, William bought second hand big American cars, such as a Chrysler or a Dodge, and stripped the body to the chassis and built a new van body on top. This had two advantages; firstly it was cheaper, but perhaps more important the softer springing was kinder to the firm's more delicate cream cakes and other specialities.

To assist in the operation of the works at Colbran Street William got D Foulds Ltd of Colne to build a lift to carry baking sheets from the ground floor to the first floor – it was the first lift made by Foulds who today are known throughout the world for their lifts.

A three course lunch could be had for 2 shillings at their cafe/restaurant which was on the first two floors at 29 Scotland Road and above the shop at 27 Scotland Road. There was a huge choice on the menu and at tea time an a la carte

menu was available – for the next 30 years all sorts of functions were held here. At one of their three cafes in Nelson, on the second floor, Nelson Rotary Club met for their weekly meeting. They also had two cafes in Burnley, one above the Savoy Cinema – this was a favourite of the present managing director Bill Oddie, grandson of the founder, and his brother, David. When their parents took them there for tea, while their mother and father finished their meal, the two lads would slip away into the cinema and the usherette would allow them to watch the film from the back row!

In 1940 William bought the arcade building on Market Street, Colne and although the building was later sold, Oddie's still retain the ground floor shop. Sadly Jane Oddie died in 1944, aged only 61. She had been a driving force behind the creation and development of the business, controlling the shops and cafes and being behind many of the firms catering successes in the 1920s and 1930s.

Two further shops were opened in the 1950s, one at Duke Bar and the other at Brierfield, but by the end of the decade all the cafes had been shut down. They had become too labour intensive and some people would stay all day, chatting over one cup of tea.

Bill Oddie, born 1941, joined the company in 1960 after studying at the Manchester Bakery College; his brother, David, born 1945, also joined the company for a short time but left to concentrate on drama education in Cornwall. Unfortunately only four years later the founder, Bill and David's grandfather, died. Bill married Lesley Wood in 1966; her family had Thomas Lamb & Sons, a fruit and vegetable wholesale business in Accrington. Their daughter, Lara Jane, was born in 1968 and about 18 months later they also had a son, Jeremy Dean. Lara has now joined the firm after studying for a marketing degree and taking business studies, while her

brother is now a quali-
fied teacher and sculptor
at Oundle School, near Peterborough.

During the 1970s the company undertook
further expansion with a first venture into a
shopping centre, the Arndale Centre in
Nelson, a shop in Coal Clough Lane in Burnley, and one at Padiham. In the 1980s they moved into the
shopping mall at Burnley, near to Marks & Spencer, and moved from their Peel Street shop into the
Accrington Arndale Centre.

In recent years the trade has changed considerably as supermarkets have opened in-store bakeries and
the shopping public have moved towards one-stop shopping. However, during this same period Oddie's
have seen a big increase in demand for lunchtime snacks and have introduced bake-off facilities so they
can provide hot pasties and pies as well as a wide range of freshly prepared sandwiches.

Throughout this decade there has been major refurbishment of the bakery with the introduction of a
new flour silo, new ovens, and other modern equipment. Following on from the 1993 success as British
Bakers of the Year, the firm once again extended their operational area by opening a shop in Blackburn
shopping precinct. In 1996 they won the much coveted Traditional Confectioner of the Year at the
British Baking Industry Awards. Compared to many organisations Oddies is still a small concern – with
13 shops and employing 200 people – but this is how Bill and Lara want it to be. This way they can stay
close to their dedicated staff and the many cus-
tomers who have come to trust
their name and products.

*Lesley Oddie
(second right)
with the cake
baked for
Charles and
Diana's
wedding in
1981*

Jean Walmsley Heap was born in Burnley at the ancient Tim Bobbin Coaching Inn. Her first attempt at clay modelling came when she was a pupil at Rosegrove Infant School, and she had her first framed picture hung when she was attending Ightenhill County Primary School. She was always pleased when friends and relations gave her sketch books or coloured pencils and drawing came naturally to her, just like breathing. At the age of ten she started selling pictures to these same friends, hoping to spend the money on a wooden hut in which she could live and paint! Her parents discouraged this idea, but permission was given for her to use the broom cupboard under the stairs, and this was called 'Studio One'.

The wooden hut where it all began and Little Thrifty

Three years later she was awarded a scholarship to Burnley School of Art where she met the distinguished painter, and her mentor, Noel H Leaver ARCA. There she resolved to become a book illustrator. With the coming of the Second World War in 1939 Jean was drafted into industry, doing leather work – any-thing from creating leather jackets to designing stuffed elephants for visiting VIPs. In 1943 she started designing large murals, which had been commissioned by the Canadian Red Cross, for children's nurseries. In 1953, Jean, then a free-lance artist, became part-time 'resident' artist in the Burnley Building Society Publicity Department. Jeannie Todd also worked at the Building Society, and she and Jean had previously met in 1950 at the Burnley Artists' Society Autumn Exhibition.

Now, in 1953, Jeannie returned starry eyed from a holiday in Scotland where she had met the famous painter John 'Lamorna' Birch and had been so inspired by him that she had promptly bought a box of paints. On her return to work she went into Jean's office asking for painting lessons. Jean was less than keen, believing that she was no teacher, but grudgingly took her sketching. The heavens opened and the thunder rolled, and they dripped back to Jeannie's house for tea and toast – and there in the garden stood the wooden hut!

Jean told Jeannie how in book illustration it was sometimes useful to make clay models of the chief characters; something which could be even

Ethel and Emily, the first volunteer part-time staff, 1955 and (right) Jean Walmsley Heap.

The first Mother Rabbit

more enjoyable than painting, but messy. Real 'clay bashing' needed a separate place .... a garden hut for instance. Within a week Jeannie's sprightly octogenarian father had cleared the hut of all its clutter, equipped it with shelves and a workbench, and in a hole in the middle of the lawn was a galvanised bin full of fine china clay.

On Coronation Day 1953, as the rain pattered on the roof, Jean sat there modelling a witch on a broomstick – the hobby had begun. The original aim was to make Christmas presents for their friends so they made equal contributions to the working capital, five pounds! Even a hobby needed a name and as they lived in the shadow of Pendle, the legendary Witch hill, 'Pendlecraft' was considered, but rejected. It was Jeannie who combined the name of the hill with the 'elfin' quality of the early models; PenDelfin was born and promptly registered.

It was decided that Jean would do the design and modelling and Jeannie would do the mould-making and casting. Initially it was a time of experimentation, of trial and error. There was no electricity in the hut and moulding had to be done in Jeannie's immaculate kitchen – soon there was the smell of boiling rubber and burnt saucepans, and even two treasured pressure cookers were ruined as the process was evolving.

After two traumatic mould-making sessions in the kitchen and an overflowing stock of materials in the hut, it was agreed that their hobby must have a home of its own. In the middle of a thunderstorm, in August 1953, they moved everything to their first studio, a small lock-up shop in Harle Syke, high above Burnley.

Jean had created a character 'Little Thrifty', who starred in her savings stories for children in the Burnley Building Society Thrifty Times, which had a circulation of 5,000 copies. There was great excitement when the Society commissioned them to produce a model of him; it was to be their largest model so far, and they started off with supreme confidence. However, everything went wrong and everywhere there was the reek of burning rubber. Little Thrifty himself ended up in three pieces and had to be stuck together with fish-glue. Their motto had been 'From small beginnings' ... it now became 'By error we progress!'

Soon the Burnley Express heard about their work and local innkeepers from Pendle Forest sought their little witch models, claiming they were the best sales gimmicks since Bury Black-Puddings! The two women were not amused.

Jim Lad and Little Mo by Dorian

Castle Tavern

Nevertheless electricity bills had to be paid and they agreed to 'sale or return' orders.

Within a few months their 'hobby' was taking all their spare time; it had become an obsession. Whilst their families saw little of them their friends at the Artists' Society were drawn to the busy little studio by the 'PenDelfin Disease'. About this time Doreen Noel Roberts, affectionately known as Dorian, joined them and eventually took charge of the small number of part-time staff. Quickly she became at home with a paintbrush and learnt their own peculiar methods, from casting and trimming, through to wrapping and packing.

They experienced difficulties with moulding some of the more intricate figures and a certain amount of hand carving had to be done to correct moulding-flaws. By 1956 they had outgrown the little shop and moved to the old Co-operative grocery store. It was ideal, for its walls were lined with shelves and long counters – there they had their nucleus of part-time staff, Ethel, Emily, Thora, Elizabeth (her husband's taxi PenDelfin's sole means of transport) and 'Duck-Ann' who came to 'try it out' and stayed for thirty-five years.

Turning the 'hobby' into a business was the next development. Greta Godbold was the first

person to take them seriously, and to prove her point took a suitcase full of samples to Kendal Milne's store in Manchester. She demanded to see the head buyer, and came back with their first 'professional' order, worth all of ten pounds! She also introduced them to Mr Rawlins, known to all the buyers in the Midlands as 'Dav'. A representative of the old school he exhibited the 'PenDelfin Range' at the International Trade Fair at Blackpool on a wobbly card table in the corner of his own stand. Now sales started to come on a proper basis and models were lovingly swathed in tissue and wrapped in newspaper; individual boxes were still years away.

It was Jean's father Henry who persuaded them it was 'make up your mind time' – should it become a full-time occupation? Henry and Jean moved into a cottage near the studio and Henry agreed to help with the moulding department; gradually he revolutionised it. New techniques allowed much greater freedom, an advantage with the period models they were making at that time. The family of rabbits was still in the future.

Creating rabbits began in a casual way – Father Rabbit, Mother Rabbit, a boy, a girl, and a rather cross little baby called Midge – but they sold, and certainly helped the girls' struggling finances. Repeat orders came pouring in and wages could be paid, but there was still much to learn. Among the new creations was a ballerina rabbit wearing a ballet skirt, named 'Margot' after Margot Fonteyn. Days took on an hilarious air; they were happy days for the whole working group was so supportive.

Financial difficulties continued to be a major concern, and it needed contributions from Jeannie's salary and from Jean's royalties from book illustration work to make ends meet. Even so, again it was removal time; they had outgrown the old Co-op. In 1958 they moved to an old mill, Oxford Mill, still up in the heights of Harle Syke. For ten pounds a week they had part of three floors, with a private lift. On the top floor they had their offices, in the middle a studio and on the ground floor packing and despatch and all the toilet facilities! Together they scrubbed the floors, singing as they scrubbed. People who had worked in the mills had developed nimble fingers and a keen eye, and they made ideal craft workers, and soon came to PenDelfin for employment.

Once again they had to move when Oxford Mill was sold, this time to single storey premises, part of Brennand Mill. It was to be their home for the next twelve years – difficult years. Again, although they had full order books, finance was the problem. They managed to avoid two takeover bids, released themselves from a well-intentioned merger, and eventually formed a limited company.

One night in 1965 Jeannie received an unexpected phone call from a Canadian over in Britain on holiday. He had just seen some of their creations and wanted to discuss Canadian and American markets. He opened the door to their first exports and later became their first export director, about the time that Dorian also became a member of the board. She had served PenDelfin in a remarkable way and now as a designer created such characters as 'The Pooch', 'Cyril Squirrel', and 'Castle Tavern', named by Dorian in honour of Barbara Castle MP, and the passing of her famous Bill against drinking and driving.

Hand casting left much to be desired, uneven texture and air holes in the mix caused models to be rejected. Whilst PenDelfin was, and is, a wholly hand-crafted product, it was only when a mixing machine was used to prepare the stoneware mix that flawless casting arrived. The man who brought about this important advance was Arthur Morley, an engineer with much experience in industrial design. He had watched the development of PenDelfin and was eventually to become its managing director.

In 1973, twenty years after those experimental days in the wooden hut, the company bought half of the refurbished Cameron Mill; it gave them 32,000 square feet of light and space, enough for their 132 workers. Situated in a less attractive part of Burnley, the site looks out onto woods and fields and Pendle Hill.

Tragedy came in 1974 when Jeannie died from cancer of the spine; her death marked the end of the first chapter of the PenDelfin story.

Now was the time to revitalise and remodel the whole range and also to move the design studio to an old Welsh farmstead. Jean, joined by Dorian and Constance, felt as if they were in heaven until the night of 11th June 1986 when they received news which completly shattered their bliss. A message came from Burnley – 'PenDelfin is burnt to the ground!' The £1 million blaze was seen for miles around, but only a week later Arthur was able to report back to Wales: 'We are back in production'. Some 10,000 feet of space at the back of the mill had been saved, and the staff brought their own tables and chairs from home to enable production to restart. They then started negotiation to buy the other half of Cameron Mill.

When the studios had been almost completely rebuilt they received a visit from Simon Towneley, the Lord Lieutenant of Lancashire. It marked a new beginning after such a disastrous event. Other new beginnings came that same year with the introduction of PenDelfin Village Tales, books requested by the many collectors of the lovable rabbits, and in 1989 the design studios were moved back north to Grange-over-Sands.

In 1992, PenDelfin's fortieth year, they launched the 'PenDelfin Family Circle', a collector's Club, which already has thousands of members worldwide.

PILKINGTON

It's difficult for us to appreciate in our light airy homes that there was a time when there was a tax on windows and people actually bricked up existing window spaces. It was as these taxes were being swept away that Pilkington became a major player in the developing glass industry.

The Pilkington family came to St Helens from Horwich, near Bolton in about 1780, and by 1826, when our story starts, were quite prosperous. That year William Pilkington took a two-elevenths share in the newly formed St Helens Crown Glass Company – the other partners were John William Bell and Thomas Bell, glassmakers, who contributed their technical expertise, John Barnes, the only solicitor in St Helens, James Bromilow, son of the main coal-owner in the town who kept the books, whilst Peter Greenall of the brewing family and William Pilkington provided capital. One of William Pilkington's sisters was Peter Greenall's wife.

However, in 1827 John William Bell was charged with evading tax on glass made at his own flintworks, and as a result the Bells pulled out of the partnership, leaving it with no technical expertise. William Pilkington, still in his

twenties, was recognised by the others as having business acumen and although he had no experience of the glass industry he took charge. He then sought the help of his elder brother Richard. Later James Bromilow and John Barnes also left. The two Pilkingtons now held eight-elevenths of the shares with their brother-in-law Peter Greenall holding the remaining three-elevenths. Fortuitously for Pilkington, three of their competitors went out of business in the next few years.

By 1834 the building market had commenced one of its cyclical upturns, and Pilkington took advantage of this by increasing their kilns to three. To sustain this growth the partners had to take out large overdrafts, and when the building boom came to a halt the banks became increasingly worried – by the end of 1842 it had reached £20,000, whereas the partnership's capital was only £26,000! Perhaps it did help that Peter Greenall's brother was a partner at Parr's Bank.

Pilkington had made crown glass, where the hot glass was spun into a circular disc, but they started making sheet glass in the early 1840s. Sheet glass was made by blowing hot glass into a long cylinder and then splitting it longitudinally, before opening and flattening it into a large rectangle; more panes could be cut from these sheets than from crown glass discs. By the late 1850s most window glass was produced by three companies – Pilkington at St Helens, Chance at Smethwick, and Hartley at Sunderland. The number of employees at Pilkington in 1849 was under 450; by 1854 this had risen to 1,350. In the 1850s Pilkington also acquired the former West works which had belonged to Mackay, and there made the cheaper rolled plate glass. However, during this period, which coincided with the repeal of window tax and glass excise duty, imports directly into London from

St Helens glassworks, 1879

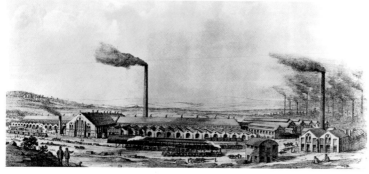

Belgium rose considerably.

During these early years substantial monies were needed for expansion and any profits had to be ploughed back into the business. They were also fruitful years for William and his wife Elizabeth for they had 14 children, of whom 12 survived infancy.

Two of each of the founders' sons became partners in Pilkington – William (Roby) and Thomas, sons of William, and William Windle and Richard, sons of Richard. During the 1860s they carried the company forward with new vigour, meeting the continental competition strongly, and even acquiring a glassworks on the continent, whilst in Britain their competitors went out of business. During the next decade Pilkington built a new factory at Cowley Hill, St Helens to manufacture polished plate glass, which became very profitable. The works were kept up to date as new technology produced new equipment and methods of working – a lehr was installed in 1904, so that glass could be annealed in four hours rather than the previous four days.

However, foreign competition in plate glass brought prices tumbling, and sheet glass profits had to support the other. In 1901 Pilkington acquired Ravenhead from the British Plate Glass Company, one of the pioneers of plate glass production. The company had been an exporter of glass for several years, had opened a warehouse in Montreal in 1892, followed by a whole network of warehouses in Canada. Soon they also had representatives in the Far East, Australia, New Zealand and South America. Between 1874 and 1894 the company's capital had grown from £150,000 to £1,400,000 – they had become a private limited company, but there was no room for or need of non-family shareholders. By 1914 a further £3 million had been ploughed back into the company.

Throughout the previous quarter century the company had introduced medical services for the employees, their wives and daughters. Even earlier they had provided facilities for cricket, rugby and bowls, a skittle alley, and a building where members could play billiards, draughts and other games. As early as about 1850 Pilkington ran a free school for boys employed by them – they either attended classes in their own time, or during the day if they had the consent of their

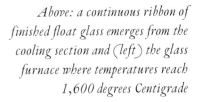

Above: a continuous ribbon of finished float glass emerges from the cooling section and (left) the glass furnace where temperatures reach 1,600 degrees Centigrade

managers or foremen; Pilkington's School was taken over by the St Helens Local Education Authority early this century. Whilst they were good employers in many ways, they ensured that the staff 'knew their place' – the directors were the bosses and would not tolerate unions.

At the start of the First World War Pilkington was employing about 10,000 people, and despite a high level of re-investment in the company, there was still a generous surplus for the shareholders. All the second generation partners left substantial fortunes.

Although the demand for plate glass in the 1920s and 1930s was not affected by the great depression the company did not capitalise on this situation – extra demand for glass came from the building of council houses and increased car production – indeed some decisions were made which cost the company a lot of money.

However, new successful processes were introduced, including the American Libbey-Owens process and the Belgian Fourcault system – both techniques basically drew glass out of a tank in a wide ribbon which passed through the remaining processes before it was cut and sent to the warehouse. Over the next few years, the management failed to take appropriate decisions on re-equipping and it wasn't until the early 1930s that Pilkington plate glass once again became competitive; there were even problems with plate glass, which had been so profitable.

During the inter-war years Pilkington did accept union participation. There was a good relationship and as a result few labour difficulties.

Several members of the family died early and others retired on health grounds, leaving an intolerable burden on the remaining three, and in 1931 an executive committee was set up involving senior managers from within the company. Two members of this team were Edward Herbert Cozens-Hardy and Ronald Morce Weeks. Edward, whose sister had married Austin Pilkington, was

Group HQ, St Helens

an eminent electrical engineer; his father, a Master of the Rolls, had been created Baron Cozens-Hardy and Edward inherited the title in 1924. Ronald joined Pilkington straight from Cambridge, as a technical trainee, and after a distinguished military service in the First World War was appointed manager of the Cowley Hill plant and eventually a director of the company. During the Second World War he became Deputy Chief of the Imperial General Staff and later Chairman of Vickers Ltd, continuing to serve Pilkington as a non-executive director until his death in 1960. In 1956 he was created Baron Weeks of Ryton.

As the fourth generation family members joined the company, there was no automatic management place for them, and each one had to take part in a rigorous assessment process; this was no mere formality and one member failed to make the grade and left the company! Among this generation was Harry Pilkington who was chairman from 1949-1973, and who was elevated to the peerage and became Lord Pilkington in 1968. He became an important national figure in industry, representing the company on various committees; eventually he became chairman of the Federation of British Industries, now the CBI, and a director of the Bank of England. However, others were not family members, but became important decision makers, particularly in budgetary control.

New developments for the company came with various takeovers, such as the production of optical glass and glass fibres; they also acquired a majority interest in Triplex (Northern) Ltd, makers of safety glass. Some of these interests and developments were also passed on to other Pilkington plants around the world.

In 1970 Pilkington went public and within a decade was finding itself under pressure from powerful institutional shareholders who were looking for regular good returns on their investments.

Lionel Alexander Bethune (Alastair) Pilkington came into the company by an extraordinary set of circumstances. A family shareholder started to investigate the Pilkington family tree and contacted Colonel Lionel Pilkington in Reading. Although unable to find a link, the two discussed the rising generation and Colonel Pilkington mentioned that his son was completing a Mechanical Sciences tripos at Cambridge University and in two years time would be looking for a job. Would Pilkington be interested?

Richard Pilkington was rebuked by the directors for this very irregular introduction, but after checking on his family and business background Alastair was taken on as a potential family director, although the family link was at least 15 generations back!

He started work in August 1947 and soon became involved in experimental work and subsequently invented the float glass process. As various openings occurred Alastair received early promotions and in 1953 joined the executive committee at a time when Pilkington was starting to become a truly international company with interests in South Africa, Canada, Australia, Argentina and Hindustan, and later in Europe.

Alastair's process was to float a ribbon of glass down a bath of molten tin, through a temperature gradient starting at 1,000 deg C and ending at about 600 deg C, after which it could be carried forward on rollers. The engineering team explored its potential, the experiments being given the initials 'LAB project', Alastair's initials. It was a complicated process, for the surface of the tin had to be kept absolutely level and the atmosphere above it completely neutral. The scientists, realising the extreme difficulties, predicted failure, but now that Alastair had a seat on the board, he could plead its case at the highest level. He was a superb advocate and an inspiration to the development team.

The success of float glass put the company in a strong position, but Sir Harry did not wish to exploit the welfare of others and instead entered into licence arrangements with other manufacturers, on the understanding that any improvements the licencees might make would be available to Pilkington. The development of float glass has ensured the company's present supremacy among the world's leading glassmakers.

Planar glass, Judiciary Square,
Washington DC

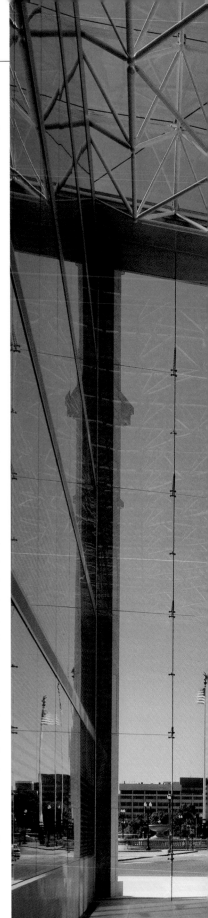

REDMANS

Albert and Thomas Redman were the sons of Thomas and Sarah Ellen Redman who lived at Lowerhouse on the outskirts of Burnley. Their father worked in a local cotton mill and the whole family, which included seven children, lived in a two up, two down terrace house. Neither Albert nor Thomas wanted to work in a mill and both started their working life at Padiham Co-op in the Grocery Department.

Albert joined the staff of the Co-op in 1896, when he was not quite thirteen years old, but on 23 March 1901 he left to take another job at the Co-

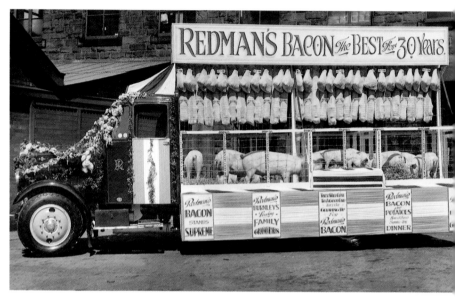

op in Colne – it gave him an increase in wages of six shillings a week, making a total of seventeen shillings a week!

Thomas Redman, the younger brother, born in 1888, started at Padiham Co-op on 12 September 1901, at six shillings a week. However, within six years, in May 1907, he opened his first very small shop at 211 Padiham Road, Burnley, specialising in bacon and cooked meats. In 1909 they opened a bacon stall in Burnley Market Hall (today Redmans are the only original market tenants) and made it a huge success. During the First World War when bacon was rationed, Redmans supplied 6,000 registered bacon customers in Burnley each week and the 'bacon queues' and 'jam queues' of 1917 were long remembered by local folk. After the First World War more shops were opened and by 1928, when they celebrated their 'coming of age', the chain had grown to a total of 80 outlets, a mix of high street shops and permanent shops in market halls. Back in 1907 they were selling 50lbs of bacon weekly and this had risen to 200lbs by 1910. However, by 1928 it had risen to 27 tons a week! The red fascias of Redman's stalls became a familiar sight throughout Lancashire and Yorkshire.

Albert also had his own shops, with the same fascias and similar trading approach, but specialising in dried fruits and nuts. He expanded much more quickly than Thomas, moving to the Manchester area, but when difficult times came there was a family concern for each other and Thomas gave financial support in exchange for shares in Albert's company.

In 1937 best prunes cost 8d lb, Lancashire cheese 1s lb, finest smoked bacon 1s 5d lb, finest Danish butter 1s 2d lb, and Redman's boiled ham 7d a quarter lb. Redmans also had bonus lines, customers being reminded to save the labels which would be exchanged for wonderful presents – such offers were available on special packs of tea, jellies, margarine, self raising flour and soap. They also offered a daily delivery service.

Two years later, in 1939, they were offering their ready cooked puddings, in seven flavours, at 2d each, suet dumpling mixture, Redman's potato crisps, and Redman's puff pastry.

Over the years the company has had great flexibility in its approach, often operating slightly different policies and prices from branch to branch, responding to local trading conditions and always working to create customer loyalty. It has also known flexibility of ownership and staff as branches have changed hands within the family group, without their customers being aware of it.

This customer loyalty was extended to Blackpool when the family opened the Redman's Park House Hotel in the town. Many customers

were pleased to take their annual holiday with the people they trusted for their weekly groceries.

In 1961 the turnover of the shops and stalls was almost £4.5 million and by 1970 this had risen to £7.5

million; the freehold and leasehold value of the properties in 1970 was estimated at a market value of £1.6 million. As trading conditions have changed, particularly with the growth of supermarkets, many shops and stalls have been disposed of, although the new owners have recognised the value of the Redman name and have continued to trade under the familiar fascia. Today Chris and his son Timothy Redman continue to operate the familiar stall in Burnley market, still offering their long famous line, high quality bacon, as well as cooked meats and a range of other fine foods.

In the 1920s weekly messages were sent down to the staff, such as:

'A Manager's place is in the shop, directing and watching the serving of customers, and cutting all the Bacon, both for counter customers and the Family Orders. Our best Managers are those who cut all the Bacon themselves.'

'No firm can exist if their customers are here today and gone tomorrow. Our best Managers and Assistants are those who recognise that it is the "repeat orders" that count rather than the immediate sale.'

'You can't be summoned for killing Bluebottles, you can for selling maggots as "Best Ham" at 2/2 per lb.'

DO YOUR PART. T.Redman & Co.

WILLOW MILLS
ACCRINGTON
LANCS. ENGLAND

ACCRINGTON WORKS

'The best tempered man in the world is the man who plays billiards. He is used to disappointment with things attempted on the table that he learns not to grumble. A billiard table in the home is the finest cure for a grumbling husband. You can have a billiard table to place on your dining room table delivered at your house from £3.17s 6d, or in easy payments from 5s 6d a month.'

Commenting on girl games, a writer in the Ladies Pictorial remarks 'In view of the fact that billiard-playing is peculiarly calculated to induce grace of movement in the growing girl, it is urged that a billiard-table should be in use in all schools and in all families where young people are being trained.' These are both extracts from 1906 advertisements placed by E J Riley Ltd, of Willow Billiard Works, Accrington, to encourage the playing of billiards in the home.

Edward John Riley was born in Accrington, one of four sons and two daughters of a cotton manufacturer. He started his working life at the Manchester and Liverpool District Bank in Accrington and was afterwards promoted to its head office in Manchester where he attained a position of considerable responsibility. However, he longed for the day he would have his own

sports shop, and in the 1870s he opened a shop in Abbey Street, between the top of Peel Street and Blackburn Road in Accrington, and later others in the Manchester area, trading under the name of Northern Athletic Supply Co. At this time he also had a workshop in Bold Street where he made bats and other sports items.

Eventually Edward started manufacturing billiard tables, cricket bats, golf clubs, tennis rackets, footballs and bowls equipment in Accrington. When Edward Riley, who became widely known as 'E J', was at his lowest ebb the man who 'saved' him was J T Kenyon, known to everyone as 'Mr Kenyon'. Mr Kenyon went into ailing companies, revived them and made them successful, then sold them on for others to control and develop. However, he saw in his relationship with E J not only a quick turn-around but clear possibilities of great future growth and therefore decided to stay. During the 1890s the two men formed a limited company, E J Riley Ltd, and in 1896 leased Willow Mills, in Dale Street, from Accrington Corporation.

Mr Kenyon's position was unusual for he was not truly a working director, rather a consultant and financial controller who in many ways supervised 'E J', the managing director – he gave E J instructions, and E J translated them into action.

E J had great energy and an inexhaustible flow of ideas on how to get rich quick; Mr Kenyon, on the other hand, has been described as 'shrewd, logical and tough'. The latter prepared a notice, and signed it, stating not only the dates of the annual holidays, but adding 'If any man is dissatisfied with his wage or conditions of work he need not come back'. Similarly tough in the 1930s, he instructed E J to get the works manager to pay off all the men. The manager resisted this, knowing that they had a lot of work in hand, but it seems Mr Kenyon was not going to sign another wage cheque until they got some money in the bank. If E J spent too little time in the accounts office, as was frequently the case, nobody else chased the debtors.

Billiards at Home

Riley's "Combine" Billiard & Dining Table

Initially the company started into billiards by selling undersized slate bed tables, made for them by Orme & Son, well known billiard table manufacturers in Manchester. However, when they discovered that the small tables had a ready sale, primarily through their own sports shops, they starting making their own and by about 1910 the company was making 800 full-sized billiard tables, and 4,000 'portable' billiard tables, which were sold by mail order, each year. They took out a patent for the combined billiard and dining table, versatile where the family had not room for a separate billiard table. They also made a 'combination couch', which could be turned into a billiard table – it is interesting that many early billiard tables were made by cabinet makers at the same time as they made the rest of the furniture for the home.

The company also became the world's largest manufacturer

of cricket bats, advertising that they had 50,000 bats in stock, each being seasoned for six months before being put on sale. They were the first to sell autographed bats; the autograph was not stamped on the bat ... the selected player came to the works, was presented with a fountain pen and signed the agreed number of bats. They also produced 1,500 bats a day, of the sort used by young families on the beach.

In 1912 E J Riley became chairman and managing director of Norbreck Hydro. In his private life E J was quite a keen amateur sportsman, being a billiard and tennis player of no mean achievement, and also enjoyed a round of golf.

During the early years of the century, Riley's used in their advertisements the phrase 'Keep your Boys at Home'. However, during the First World War this phrase got them into trouble as officers of the Ministry of Defence thought they were trying to encourage young men to become conscientious objectors, and they had to quickly remove the slogan from their vans!

The three shops in Manchester were retained until the early 1920s; at this time the company also had about 40 billiard halls – they were prosperous years.

Edward J Riley, who lived at South View, Whalley Road, Accrington, died in 1925, aged 70, but by that time his company had become the largest builder of billiard tables in the world, and also owned forty billiard halls in Britain.

After the Second World War the company bought C D Pierce & Son Ltd furniture manufacturers, and later acquired Stevens & Mercer Ltd who manufactured chair frames for C D Pierce & Son Ltd.

In 1967 E J Riley Ltd bought the billiard table repair side of Burroughs and Watts, and Riley Burwat Ltd was born. This gave them a network of branches throughout the British Isles, but some of these were later closed.

A few years later Modern Recreations Ltd was formed to bring together the billiard halls, later called billiard clubs, owned by Riley's and Burroughs and Watts; these eventually became Riley Snooker Clubs Ltd.

Today Riley Leisure, now based in Burnley, are recognised as the world's premier manufacturer of cue sport products, including billiards, snooker and pool. They supply tables for all the ranking tournaments, across the world, organised by the World Professional Billiards and Snooker Association, and also supply 120,000 cues a year.

The company is now part of the Hainsworth group of companies, Hainsworth's manufacturing the fine green cloth which adds the finishing touch to all the engineering and skill of a century's experience in producing match-winning tables.

Riley Leisure sponsor major players, including Stephen Hendry, who has a long association with the company. So when you turn on your television and watch those balls, seemingly, disappear down your throat, they are speeding across a Riley Aristocrat Tournament table, one of the 14,000 products of this company which might have failed had it not been for the help of 'Mr Kenyon', but which is now a world beater.

H.SAMUEL

The Samuel family were part of Breslau's flourishing Jewish community in the 18th century. At that time Breslau was part of Austria, and Menachem (the Jewish word for comforter), later to be called Emanuel, had to flee to Posen in Poland, settling in the town of Kempen on the Silesian border. His grandson, called Emanuel after his grandfather, came to London in 1775.

He had three sons and a daughter – the ones of interest to us were Louis Samuel who was born in 1794 and became a watchmaker and silversmith in Liverpool, and his brother Moses, born 1795, who was an author and watchmaker in the city in the early part of the 19th century. Moses was a Hebrew scholar, authority on rabbinical literature and a zealous advocate of Jewish emancipation. The brothers were of sufficient repute to feature in Watchmakers and Clockmakers of the World, and a clock made by them in 1824 was still keeping time almost 150 years later in the directors' dining room at H Samuel. In 1819 Louis married Henrietta, whom he had first met when she opened the door to him (still in hair curling papers) at the home of his friend Harry Alexander Israel in London, and in 1821 Moses married Harriet; they were both daughters of Israel.

Moses' son Walter, who was born in 1829, married Harriet the daughter of Shreiner Wolfe. Walter only survived his father by 18 months, dying in 1863. That same year Harriet started a small jewellery and watchmaking business at 103 Market Street, Manchester, which also sold watches by mail order. This could have been a continuation of the Liverpool firm, and at least one of their children was born in Liverpool. The company is named 'H Samuel' after Harriet.

Walter and Harriet had five children – daughters Evelyn, Florence and Lucille and sons Arthur Harrington Samuel and Edgar Samuel, who was born in 1861, but who in 1896 changed his name to Edgar Samuel Edgar. The Market Street premises became the firm's first headquarters. It was Edgar who at first helped his mother in the business, and later formed a partnership with her. Edgar was very progressive and significantly developed the business, opening a branch in Preston, and then others throughout Lancashire, before it become a national chain of shops. The partnership was dissolved in 1891, leaving Edgar in charge of the business. Harriet died in 1908.

Edgar and his wife Ethel had three children – Gilbert, Robert and Margaret.

In 1912 Edgar decided to establish a new headquarters and factory in Hunters Road, Birmingham – so that the business would be

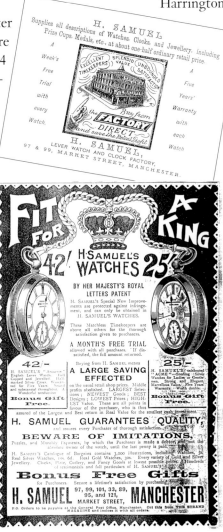

Ads from 1887 Jubilee (top) and Strand magazine 1899

in the heart of the city's jewellery quarter. This first factory was built to his own design and had many advanced features, and also contained the head office of the mail order company. By 1911 H Samuel were encouraging readers of The Christian Herald and Signs of our Times to send a postcard for a copy of 'H Samuel's magnificent FREE BOOK OF 3000 BARGAINS – a book that is absolutely indispensable in laying out money to the best advantage. Thousands have saved enormously by making use of it. GET THE BOOK AT ONCE and study its wealth of bargain offers in Watches, Jewellery, Plate, Cutlery.

Pages from a catalogue circa 1906. Below: the shop in Tavern Street, Ipswich.

Full month's trial allowed. FREE PRIZES.' A popular advertisement of the day stated 'Every pillar box is a branch of H Samuel!'

In 1917 Edgar converted the firm into a private limited company, H Samuel Ltd, of which he became life governing director, a position he held until his death in 1933. The First World War started shortly after the factory opened, and plans for major expansion had to wait until 1918, when peace returned. In 1935 the directors added a second factory, which was designed to incorporate improved working conditions, particularly to provide light rooms, so essential for the manufacture and repair of jewellery and watches.

In the 1930s the company was claiming 'H.Samuel shops cover the Kingdom – Come to your nearest Branch, Thousands of Factory Bargains await You!' At that time the company, in addition to selling jewellery, clocks and watches, was also selling umbrellas, binoculars, musical instruments, gramophones and records. An advertisement proclaimed that an 'Everite King' watch had been thrown from Big Ben, from scaffolding at a height of 250 feet, on 3 August 1933, when not even the glass was broken or the case dented and 'it never even stopped'. Similar tests with watches fixed to channel swimmers and the front of express trains brought more publicity – and presumably more sales.

Year by year new branches were opened and once again extensions to the factory were planned, but the start of the Second World War delayed these ambitious plans. Instead

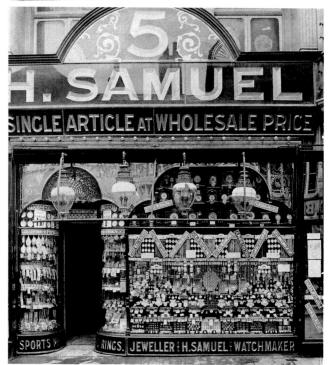

they turned to making parts for tanks, as part of the war effort!

After the war in 1945 a third factory was built in Birmingham; the architect had visited Switzerland to see innovative ideas in the 'land of the watch'. All the factories were interconnected.

In 1947 Mr Edgar was looking for a designer and craftsman jeweller to join the company, when he saw a coffee pot which he very much liked. On asking who had designed and crafted it he was told it was a young man called Frank Neville. At that time Frank had been offered a post in New York but was persuaded to stay when he was assured that Mr Edgar would make the contacts and Frank would be allowed total freedom in design and craftsmanship. It was the start of a life long dedication to Samuel's and during that time he designed a fruit bowl as a present to mark the Silver Wedding of Queen Elizabeth and the Duke of Edinburgh, a goblet for the Queen Mother, and many sporting trophies. One special commission was to design and craft a replacement World Cup Trophy after the original was stolen, but this trophy was never made – because a dog found the stolen one!

Efforts were always made to recover all fragments of gold left on workers' hands, clothes, shoes or carpets – the hand washing water passed through a sieve and the gold remains were extracted.

In 1948 H Samuel became a limited company, with shares floated on the Stock Exchange, but these were mainly held by members of the family. Further shares, A Ordinary Shares, were issued in 1953 but these carried no voting rights, and therefore the family

Thirties catalogue and 1938 shop window showing Everite watches

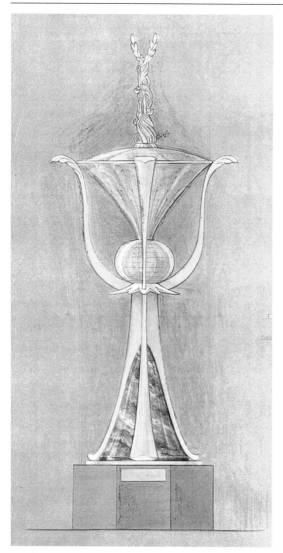

A design for the World Cup which was never needed

still continued to exercise control of the company. About this time H Samuel not only had about 200 people employed on watch and clock repairs but also had made their own brand cutlery in Sheffield. The company also sponsored many sporting events, including channel swimmers; it was all good publicity.

In the 1960s the company acquired 'Watches of Switzerland of New Bond Street', selling watches which were of very high quality; this company was later sold to Asprey by Gerald Ratner.

Edgar's sons, Gilbert and Robert, became directors and served the company into the late 1970s. Gilbert, who was educated at Charterhouse, became chairman and joint managing director of H Samuel in 1935, and was elected a member of the Worshipful Company of Clockmakers. He also became High Sheriff of London. His brother Robert was the other joint managing director. Later Robert's son Anthony Samuel Edgar and Gilbert's son-in-law Stephen Gentilli became directors. Stephen's son Adam also joined the company, going to Germany and Switzerland to learn the art of jewellery crafting and watchmaking, before becoming a director.

In 1984 H Samuel took over James Walker, a jewellery company based in Streatham which had branches in the London area.

In 1986 H Samuel were taken over by the Ratner Group plc and ceased to be under the control of the family of Harriet Samuel.

1898 100 YEARS 1998
OF SWEET SUCCESS
UNCLE JOE'S MINT BALLS
KEEP YOU ALL AGLOW

WILLIAM SANTUS & CO. LTD.

Most Lancashire folk have not only heard of Uncle Joe's Mint Balls, but have tasted them and come back for more. However, their fame has

William Santus counting sweet coupons during rationing in the 1940s

in recent years spread through-out Britain and there have even been reportings of them having rolled as far as Vancouver and New York!

The founder of the company was William Santus, who was born in 1873, one of seven children. It was a family that knew poverty, their father being a shot firer at the local colliery; they lived at 73 Platt Lane, Scholes, an area then known as St Catherine's Ward.

William left school when he was fourteen. What his first job was we do not know, but in 1898 he bought stall 125 in the New Market Hall in Wigan.

He married a local dressmaker, Ellen Seddon, at Greenough Street Independent Methodist Church at the beginning of the same year, and from the marriage licence we gather that he was a fruit and potato dealer.

They made their home at 6 Acton Street, in Wigan.

The Seddon family were great friends with the Atty family who were well established in the confectionery trade, and it is likely that it was they who taught Ellen the art of toffee making. Selling sweets was initially a sideline for the Santus's, a few sweets sold on the corner of his fruit stall, but within a few years they had become the only thing William sold.

By 1908 William owned stalls in Bolton and St Helens, as well as the one at Wigan. The sweets had become extremely popular and the tiny kitchen of the home in Acton Street could no longer meet the demand. William realised it was time to expand and formed the 'Swinley Confectionery Company', the couple going into partnership with William's brother-in-law J J Fortune, a charismatic Wiganer. He owned some property at 62 Kenyon Road, and in the shadow of the huge Rylands Cotton Mill, they built a small domestic factory. There they started manufacturing their mint balls and treacle toffees, among other well loved sweets.

William sold the stalls in Bolton and St Helens and concentrated all his efforts in Wigan. The sweets were taken from the factory to the market on a small truck, by a young lad called Eric. He got up early each morning and hand-wrapped all the sweets he had to deliver before going to Wigan Grammar School, all for a few shillings a week and as many sweets as he could eat – a young lad's dream! This arrangement lasted for about six years, but once again demand exceeded production capacity and another move became necessary.

In 1919 work started on a new factory in Dorning Street, off Wallgate; the same building in which the company is based today. The Wigan Observer of the time stated: 'The firm are to be congratulated on their enterprise in embarking on their new development as it will find employment for a considerable number of people.' The factory cost £2,400 to build, but about that time Mr Fortune decided to retire,

and the firm became William Santus and Company.

Production increased and new workers were needed, but they had to meet William's two basic criteria – that they already knew someone who worked at the factory, and they had to be Methodists. This informal policy, he believed, meant that there was always a friendly and happy atmosphere in the factory. We are told that he was a good boss, firm but fair, but the workers had a healthy respect for his temper!

A lady called Margaret Carter produced the first mint ball in the new factory in 1921 – she also boiled Mr Santus's egg for lunch each day.

Staff worked from 8am to 6pm, Monday to Friday; they also worked on Saturday mornings, when the factory was scrubbed down from top to bottom; pans were cleaned with rubbing stones, caramel pans and the floors were scraped and scrubbed to get rid of the toffee which had splashed and hardened. Other jobs included winching the sweets upstairs in a bucket, to be hand-wrapped. Although William Santus was the managing director he still continued to help with production almost up to his death, his speciality being the making of treacle toffee.

In 1933 Uncle Joe's Mint Balls were patented and the firm became a registered company in 1937. William now put his mind to advertising his mint balls more widely, particularly encouraging people to sample them. Samples were distributed to men queueing in the cold outside football and rugby grounds, including those of Manchester United and Stockport Town, whilst inside the

grounds packets were on sale; these in turn contained a sample packet with one mint ball printed with the slogan 'Take this home for the kiddie.' The tradition of eating Uncle Joe's Mint Balls at football matches started in this way, for they really did, and do, provide 'internal heating'! Women were given samples as they stood in cinema queues, whilst children outside school gates were given sample packets which bore the message 'Go and ask Mother for a penny'; there was also a message for mother explaining why Uncle Joe's Mint Balls are so good for youngsters. So dedicated was William Santus to establishing his new company that on Saturday nights he personally visited local pubs distributing free packets of mint balls; he also wrote all the newspaper and cinema advertisements himself.

The war years could have been devastating, not only because of rationing, but also because staff were called away to fight. The worst effect of this was in 1942 when Tommy Bennett, their only remaining sugar boiler, was called up; Mr Santus had to write to the Ministry of Labour for special exemption, but this was only granted until a woman had been trained to fulfil his duties.

Olive Jameson on the old market stall, 1939

In 1952 the company was commissioned to make 19,400 ounces of soft centre fruit sweets to be used to fill Coronation mugs, which were then

The company enters the international market in 1998

given to schoolchildren aged from five to eleven. The company held social occasions for the staff and in 1952 the Wigan Observer reported on one such evening, which was held at Kendal Street Methodist Church, where a meal of Lancashire hotpot, cakes, and trifle was served, before games and community singing completed the event.

William Santus continued to run the company until his death in 1953. In his later years he had moved to live in Southport but was brought to the factory every morning in his chauffeur driven Daimler. William and Ellen only had one child, Nellie, who never recovered from her father's death. She died on his birthday three years later at the early age of 51, whilst her mother lived on until 1964. On each death the company suffered from the impact of large death duties.

The responsibility for rebuilding and developing the company passed to Frank Winnard, Ellen's nephew, and to his son John Winnard Snr, and his sons Antony and John. John Winnard Snr died

suddenly in 1990 and although the next generation were already deeply involved in the manufacturing side of the business, they were only just beginning to develop an understanding of company management. They realise, however, the importance of ensuring their sweets have that magical old fashioned appeal and they insist on using the traditional gas fires to boil the sugar and other ingredients. They also value the skills of the staff who handmake the sixty different types of sweets produced today. It is only such operations as wrapping and packing and despatch that have been modernised.

But who was 'Uncle Joe'? The honest answer is.... we don't know. Some believe he was one of the Atty family, but no sign of Joe is present in their family tree. It looks as if our genial, aristocratic friend is after all fictional, a figment of someone's imagination – but who knows?

Today the Mint Balls are made in exactly the same way that Ellen Santus made them in her tiny kitchen, but now they are wrapped by machine. The recipe is a secret, known only to the current managing directors, brothers Antony and John Winnard. From as early as 1200BC mint has been used for its refreshing, healing, and even mystical powers and today mint essence is still one of the main ingredients of Uncle Joe's Mint Balls.

SHEARINGS

Herbert Shearing was born in 1888 in the village of Hapton – not near Burnley, but about twelve miles south-west of Norwich. He was the middle one of the five children of Samuel and Rachel Shearing.

He decided to join the Royal Navy and served at HMS Shotley near Ipswich, but was later discharged due to a heart condition which was brought on by an accident to his chest.

He and his wife Nellie moved to live in Lancashire about 1914, where he opened a small garage in Lees Road, Oldham. Sadly Nellie died, but he later married Elsie Jackson, and in the 1920s started Shearings Tours Ltd. Elsie was a skilled shorthand typist and she looked after the bookings and administration whilst Herbert built up the fleet and all the practical arrangements.

Herbert Shearing

By the 1930s Shearings Tours Ltd held numerous touring licences, which had to be obtained from the Traffic Commissioners. The company ran tours to Scotland, the Norfolk Broads, Wales and the Wye Valley, Cornwall, and North and South Devon. Over the years Torquay became the most popular destination and Herbert Shearing bought the Burlington Hotel on Torquay's Babbacombe Road. Those staying at the hotel knew that they would be looked after by Shearings staff throughout their holiday. In the mid 1930s Herbert built a new 60 bed hotel in Torquay, which he named the Dorchester – this was a private hotel and was not used in conjunction with the tours. Later in about 1944 he also bought the Devonshire Hotel.

Back in Oldham during this period Herbert created a partnership, Shearing & Crabtree – it was a coach building company based in Moorhey Street – and there they built the coachwork on Leyland and Bedford chassis for the Shearings coaches.

During the war almost all the coaches were requisitioned by the War Office. Late in 1944 Herbert's health deteriorated due to the heart condition with which he had been discharged from the Royal Navy all those years before, and Shearings was sold to Ripponden and District Motors in 1945. Herbert died later that year, aged 57.

Over the years other companies have become

Smith's Pagefield charabanc in 1921 about to depart from Wigan for Blackpool

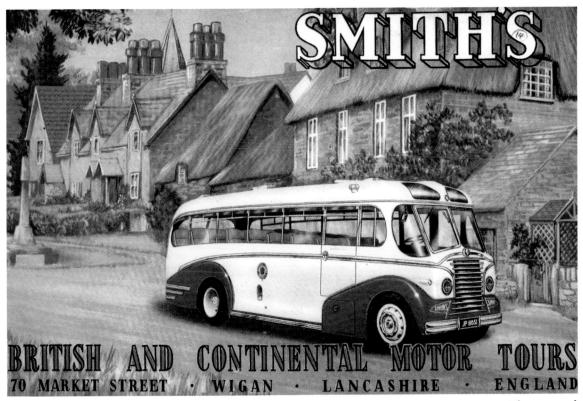

SMITH'S

BRITISH AND CONTINENTAL MOTOR TOURS
70 MARKET STREET · WIGAN · LANCASHIRE · ENGLAND

part of the modern Shearings. A company was started by William Webster in 1903, who in addition to carrying passengers also operated a haulage and removals business. Another company was commenced in 1914 by James Smith and that year his company ran a tour to John O'Groats – both companies operated from Wigan.

By 1935 'Webster's Tours' were operated by the Smith company and the first continental tour was offered in 1938. They also claimed to be the first company to resume such tours after the war, taking tourists to Switzerland for 14 days. For the Channel crossings the coach was hoisted by ropes onto the Southern Railway ferry boat.

Following the company's purchase by Les Gleave in 1958, it became Smith's Tours (Wigan) Ltd, but continued to show the well known 'Smith's Ivory' livery. By now the group of companies owned by Gleave had extensive cover of the north west and North Wales. Soon the company was becoming involved in transporting sports teams, and became the carrier of the Great Britain, Australian, New Zealand, and French Rugby League teams.

Wilf Blundell started his working life as a butcher, before buying a taxi, and in 1950 getting his first coach, a Bedford OB with a Duple Vista body. Gradually he built up his fleet of coaches and in 1964 acquired Smith's and Webster's from Les Gleave. The combined fleet now reached 55 coaches and following the take over of Hargreaves Coaches (Bolton) Ltd, with its 12 coaches, the Blundell Group's first holiday hotel was purchased – the Belle Vue at

The company's oldest surviving brochure (below right) and sixties letterhead. Smith's brochure 1951 (above) showing a Leyland Tiger

Spencer and Auty

"Down South" Tour.

Special Inclusive Fare £9 9s.

Motor Chara Proprietors,
Kingsley Works, Brook Street,
Bury.

'Phone 643 Bury.

Shearings Tours
(MANCHESTER) LTD

OLYMPIA COACH STATION
LIVERPOOL STREET
SALFORD·5, LANCS

Eastbourne. Other hotels joining the group were the Grantham Astor and the Southdown, both in Eastbourne; by 1980 the group had nine hotels in locations from Scotland to Cornwall. Other holiday tour operators acquired by Blundell's were Sandown Camping Holidays of Burnley and William Hartley (Tours) Ltd of Manchester. In 1968 Wilf Blundell took control of both Happiday Tours Ltd of Manchester and Stanley Spencer's Tours of Manchester. He changed the name to Happiway-Spencers Ltd, and from 1975 the name Smiths Happiway-Spencers was used. However, sadly, Wilf Blundell died in 1978, aged 55.

At the end of 1982 the vehicles were lettered 'Smiths Happiways'. Following the deregulation of the coaching industry the company bought Kildare Coaches Ltd, which gave them a presence in the Doncaster area, and General Omnibus Services Ltd of Chester-le-Street, which gave them an opening in County Durham. In 1953, James Robinson had bought Shearings Tours Ltd and in 1963 he formed Shearings Holidays Ltd. In 1964 Jacksons of Altrincham Ltd acquired Shearings Holidays Ltd, making it the earliest root of the Shearing family, for great-grandfather Jackson in the 19th century worked horse-drawn coal wagons, which at weekends were converted into coaches!

Other companies came into the fold over the next few years, including Salopia Saloon Coaches Ltd, which gave them a presence in the West Midlands and in 1982 the firm became simply 'Shearings Holidays'.

However, it was only two years later that Associated Leisure took over Shearings Holidays Ltd, bringing together the two historic strands – Shearings and Smith's – but within a few weeks they had been taken over by Pleasurama PLC and later that year moved their headquarters to the present site in Miry Lane, Wigan. After the two companies had come together, they had a fleet of 294 vehicles.

In 1986 Pleasurama PLC bought National Holidays, a subsidiary of National Bus Company – however, it had no buses, but was a marketing and administration organisation, used to working with 'feeder' companies which gave Smith Shearings access to national coverage and a greatly increased passenger potential. It also gave them the right to use the famous National Holidays logo and the white, red and blue livery, but in 1989 the company decided to change its name to Shearings National. At this time the firm also became involved in providing local bus services, and eventually operated in many parts of the north west as well as in Barnsley, and Neath in South Wales.

About this time Pleasurama was taken over, in a reverse bid, by the smaller Mecca Leisure PLC, who already owned Warners holiday centres, including 19 hotels, but in 1990 The Rank Organisation plc made a successful takeover of the Mecca Leisure Group with a bid of £538 million!

In 1996 the Rank Organisation decided that Shearings did not fit in with their core products. Once again, following a successful management buyout Shearings is an independent company, one of the largest coach operators in the United Kingdom.

John Spencer (Textiles) Ltd

John Spencer was a warehouse lad earning 2s 6d a week, but he dreamed that one day he would be a business magnate! Many of us dream, but our ambition often stops there. Not so with John; he became a grocer in Lanebridge in Burnley and saved every penny he could. He put his son, also John Spencer, to the trade of a weaver early in life, and for some years he was manager of Clifton Mill in Burnley. However, in 1871 John Snr started in business with his son John, and John's brother, at Waterloo Shed on Trafalgar Street, where they had 110 looms.

As the years passed orders got larger and larger, so the firm moved to Ashfield Mill, where the company is based today, before moving to Elm Street.

Primrose Day, 19 April 1887 was a great day in the firm's history, for that was the day they opened their newly-erected Queen's Mill. They were people with a great faith in the cotton industry, and although they had hard times, this faith was justified. At one stage they had over 2,000 looms – 857 at Queen's Mill and 1,276 at Imperial Mill in Rosegrove, which they had built in 1905; these were powered by a large horizontal steam engine. At the time of the jubilee of Queen's Mill, Tertius Spencer was the head of the firm; he was named Tertius because he was the third son born to his parents, the previous two having died in infancy. To celebrate the mill's jubilee he took about 800 cotton workers on two special trains to Blackpool where they were provided with tea and and free access to the Winter Gardens. Whilst there, Tertius Spencer, speaking about his employees, said 'They are grand people. I have been working with them since 1898, so I should know.'

The old mill before it was destroyed by fire with the new one (right). John Spencer (bottom right) with John Spencer Jnr and Tertius Spencer (centre)

During the early years of the century the firm largely wove a cloth used for African prints, but after the Second World War became famous for its high quality cotton shirting, manufacturing about 300,000 yards a week, and suppling many of the leading shirt manufacturers. Marks & Spencer bought a third share in the company, in return for a similar allocation of the cloth which at that time was in very short supply.

Even in the 1930s the firm was exporting cloth to many parts of the world; it was said that British needs could be woven before breakfast, the remainder of the day being given to producing for export!

In the early post-war years great-grandson John replaced 1,400 traditional Lancashire looms with 576 weaving machines; the company invested heavily in the modernisation of their machinery, but by the late 1960s it was clear that further redevelopment was again necessary. It became obvious that various shareholders felt the industry had a doubtful future and preferred to have their capital returned to them; Marks & Spencer also withdrew from the production process. In 1970 John Spencer, the third member of the family to bear the name, was awarded the OBE, not least for his work as a member of the standing consultative conference of the Industrial Research Association, and as a member of the Textile Council.

However, in 1971 the firm was wound up. The major shareholders at this time were John H Spencer who had about a 20 per cent holding, Marks & Spencer with about 33 per cent, the remainder being held by about 12 other people. Working in the business was J H Spencer, Jack Spencer, Mark Collinge, nephew of J H Spencer and David Spencer, son of Jack. J H Spencer's only son had been killed in a gliding accident, aged 17, in the 1960s, and as a

result a certain amount of dynastic impetus was lost. Tertius' grandson, Mark Collinge, was now managing director and he kept the family name alive by setting up John Spencer (Textiles) Ltd. This was no easy option for it meant Mark had to raise £60,000 share capital and secure a £20,000 overdraft from the bank — today these may not seem vast amounts but about 30 years ago it was a lot for a family business to assemble. The share capital came mainly from within the family, but the bank overdraft was more difficult to finance and meant Mark had to surrender the deeds of his house and his share certificates; he almost put everything on the line!

The old business involved the mass production of textiles to supply chain stores, the Ministry of Defence, and Local Authorities with a range of three or four basic cloths, but many of these customers started obtaining their stocks more cheaply from developing countries where labour rates were much lower. Mark Collinge bought 112 looms from the old company and decided that the firm would diversify to produce a wide range of fabrics, but not more than 10 per cent of any one particular type of cloth. He found the Burnley Corporation had Ashfield Mill empty, so quite fortuitously moved back to where his forebears had started their business, bringing with him the best of the workers from the old business. He was innovative in labour relations which was reciprocated, and all worked very hard together. He offered them a share in the company profits and also a pension scheme — benefits which at the time were probably unique in the textile industry.

The Lancashire textile trade had seen dramatic changes over the previous seventy years. In 1912 712,000 people were employed in cotton and allied textile trades; by 1982 that figure had plummeted to only 34,000. Similarly in

1912 only about 8 per cent of textiles used in this country came from abroad; by 1982 import penetration had risen to 77 per cent.

Although John Spencer (Textiles) Ltd had still only 112 looms in 1983, at any one time they could produce 45-50 different cloths. The end products ranged from cloths for the covers of books, ones upon which a PVC covering would enable them to be made into fancy aprons, tracing cloths for architect's offices, cordite bags for guns, poplin for use in hospital gowns, but also very fine poplins and linings for use by Jermyn Street tailors in expensive shirts and suits.

Mark Collinge was managing director, bought the yarn and sought orders for the finished cloths and directed production at the mill!

In 1991 a major fire engulfed the mill and everything was destroyed except one weaving shed. This became the core centre for production over the next few months, but with the money received from the insurers a modern £2.5 million mill has been developed. Mark Collinge, although chairman is semi-retired, and his son, David is now managing director of this unusual family business.

TIMPSON

The Timpson family stretch back into the history of both North Northamptonshire and South Leicestershire, as far as the 16th century.

William Timpson was born in Rothwell, in Northamptonshire, in 1849, the youngest of six children, and later married Elizabeth Farey. They had eight children – five girls and three boys, but Elizabeth died when she was 41 and William was 42. Two years later he married Katharine Mursell and they had their own family of two boys and two girls.

William was not very strong as a boy, and at quite an early age illness forced him to retire from active participation in the business he started; nevertheless he remained at the helm, not least as head of the family. Although he had little formal education William was well read, and could use quotations with ease and freedom; he was also good at figures, had a good brain, and was a great saver. When only eight he was already earning a

few coppers by making leather bootlaces, or by carrying boots from outworkers to Messrs Gotch's at Kettering, probably the founders of the boot and shoe industry in that area whose business was particularly based on army boots.

His eldest brother Charles grew to be a big man – a full six feet tall, and weighing 20 stone. In the hungry forties Charles and a friend walked to Manchester to obtain work, and many from their home area followed.

When William was about eleven it was decided to send him to Manchester to join Charles. His box of clothes was sent on ahead by carrier and he walked to Desborough station to catch the train, waving goodbye to his school chums on the way. There was no direct line and the boy ended up late in the afternoon at Sheffield station, tired and hungry – stranded.

Seeing him crying a kindly gentleman traveller took him to Manchester and paid the excess fare. Charles had come to meet him but had given him up and gone home from London Road station. The man took William by cab to Charles' home, before he disappeared into the night, never to be seen again.

Charles and his wife were not easy company and William took every opportunity to save, and gain his independence. Growing up was hard as Charles was very demanding. The young lad went to night school and became closely associated with Ashley Lane Church and Sunday School. One morning William overslept and was late for work. Charles was angry at this and threatened the lad with a cane, but William stepped back, picked up a shoe last and warned him that if he hit him he could expect the shoe last! Charles backed off, but William decided it would be better if he returned to Rothwell.

Back at Rothwell, William learned the art and craft of shoe-making – shoemakers were often

William Timpson, founder, in his early twenties

Oldham Street shop about 1896

North Park Factory which was producing 17,000 pairs of shoes by 1939

boots on a Saturday, and he served each customer himself. In his first trading year he made a clear profit of £1,000 and used the money to buy property in Withington.

At that time it was common to have running through the shop a long gas pipe fitted with dozens of jets, and from this he hung hundreds of pairs of children's shoes. Timpson's shops were usually single fronts with a side door (they had most likely been single fronted dwelling houses). In better branches the fronts were of polished mahogany, whereas the smaller ones were painted wood, but almost all had good name signs, either above or painted on the window. The interiors were also well fitted out, but most shops, having no natural light, were rather dark and dingy. The manager always wore a shoemaker's apron and the lady assistants wore black dresses. The weeks before Whitsuntide were nearly always busy as families bought new shoes for the children, ready for the Sunday School's Whit Monday walks.

regarded as superior people, who held religious and political views, and people would gather in the workshop in the evening to listen, whilst the craftsman cobbled away. The man who William worked for was one of these, and when the old man died he carried on the business for a short while. He soon discovered it could take him a week to make a pair of hand-sewn boots, but only a few minutes to sell them! Perhaps this was what led him, at the age of sixteen, in 1865, to return to Manchester and join his brother-in-law, Walter Joyce, in a partnership in a retail boot and shoe business at 298 Oldham Road.

In May 1870 William started up on his own. He rented a shop at 97 Oldham Street, near Piccadilly and the market, but even in those days he had to pay a rent of £200 a year for this one shop – to avoid ridicule he told his friends he was only paying £100. He spent all his money on shop fittings and had to obtain his stock on credit from Messrs Shaw's of Dantzic Street, boot and shoe wholesalers who knew him through his Sunday School work and trusted him implicitly. He was good at shop window displays and people travelled a good distance to see what he had to offer – often he sold a hundred pairs of men's

Salford shop in the fifties

William was about twenty-three when he married and went to live over the shop, but after a short while went to live in one of the houses he had bought at Withington. Gradually other shops were acquired, at 58 Stretford Road, 113 Oxford Road and at 26 Great Ancoats Street. The air in the shops was usually bad, mainly from the amount of gas which was used, and as a result William Timpson went to see a specialist about his health. He was told bluntly; 'Young man, I will give you a choice – either the Southern Cemetery, Manchester, or your native heath!'

Within a few months William returned to Kettering, and to a certain extent began the life of a country gentleman – he was only thirty.

At his age he wouldn't contemplate retiring – he worked out a detailed plan of how he would conduct the business. Alternate Tuesday afternoons he left for Manchester by train, returning at the weekend, which gave him ten clear days in Kettering before returning to the city. Through this arrangement he was able to rest and recuperate, but also keep a steady eye on his affairs – it was a regular feature of his life for nearly forty years. By now Kettering was a busy boot and shoe manufacturing centre and soon he was able to develop lasts which suited the feet of Manchester people and gathered together craftsmen to make footwear for his shops. By the end of 1896 Timpson's had 26 shops spread around the country; in the next six years they opened another eleven. It wasn't until 1898 that the business acquired its own horse and a lorry to service the Manchester shops.

About the turn of the century the Americans introduced half sizes; their shoes were imported to this country, as were ladies' shoes from Austria and Switzerland. Timpson's did not start manufacturing their own ladies' shoes until the beginning of the First World War, and these were mainly styles suitable for women employed on munitions work or on the trams.

William's son W H F Timpson gradually took over the development of new sites as his father's health declined further. New shops appeared in Sheffield, Nottingham, Liverpool and Leeds. William died on 23 January 1929 – at his funeral service he was described as the son of Encouragement, the man who encouraged everybody.

By the time of the Second World War Timpson's had over 200 shops, a large modern shoe factory, 30 shoe repairing factories, warehouse facilities and over 3,500 employees.

In more recent years the firm has concentrated on the shoe repair aspect of the business, and no longer sells shoes. However, it now has over 315 outlets offering shoe care, the cutting of keys, engraving and watch repairing; many of these outlets are in major city and town centres.

In recent years Timpson's has undergone several changes as many people's choice of footwear has changed from stiletto-heeled and traditional shoes, which needed regular repairing, to trainers and similar 'disposable' ones, many of which are imported. John Timpson, the chairman of Timpson's and great grandson of William, believes that high quality service by well trained friendly staff is one sure element in a market place which is changing ever more quickly. He finds it difficult to project where the firm will be in ten years time but there is within the company today a burning desire to find success, just as William showed all those years ago.

1920s showcard

John Noel Nichols (known as Noel) was born in 1883, the youngest child of John Cooke Nichols and his wife Lois. John was a yarn merchant but his son was more interested in herbs, spices and essences from around the world. He enjoyed experimenting and developed a range of flavoured fruit cordials, among them one he claimed would give those who drank it 'vim' and vigour. This was in 1908, and soon the concentrate was on the list of goods he supplied to herbalist shops and temperance bars in Manchester – it was a success from the beginning.

He set up his small business at 49 Granby Row, Manchester as a wholesale druggist and herb importer, the business apparently being financially backed by relatives. His brother Samuel and his brother-in-law Jim Stothert, a wholesale druggist, each loaned him £100.

Noel packed herbs, roots, spices and barks, along with colourings and flavourings, which herbalists could make into pills or medicated draughts. He also supplied some proprietary remedies such as nit ointment, camphor squares, pills and potions, in addition to concocting a few speciality items of his own, generally in the form of tonics. Before the days of the National Health Service, herbalists provided an essential service when many people could not afford to go to the doctor.

Noel Nichols in his first car, a Fiat 501, in 1922

In the years before the First World War many towns had their herbalist shops, which sold hot and cold tonic drinks and cordials; similarly towns had temperance bars which sold non-alcoholic drinks, an alternative to pubs and a venue for billiard rooms – they sold soft drinks (known as mineral waters) and milk drinks, instead of beers and spirits. J N Nichols and Company sold the ingredients for such well established drinks as dandelion and burdock, sarsaparilla, and herb beer. They also sold a powder called 'Thump' for milk drinks.

In 1907 The Mineral Water Trade Review drew attention to a Bill which was to go before Parliament

which would restrict the long opening hours of public houses. They felt this presented an opportunity for the creation of a branded fancy drink concentrate for sale to herbalists and temperance bars. A family friend, sixteen year old Tom Broadhurst, helped Noel Nichols in his business and no doubt did the fetching and carrying as Noel tried to create such a drink. They stirred several ingredients together in a barrel, varying the quantities until Noel got the balance of flavours just right. During the daytime Noel went round on a bicycle taking orders, and at night he mixed up the cordial according to his secret recipe, and then bottled and corked it ready for delivery the next day. Ernest Galley, who had just left school, also helped with the production. It was these three who did all the ordering of raw materials, production of the cordial, advertising, deliveries and office work.

As the business grew they moved to larger rented premises at 203A Chapel Street, Salford. It was an excellent site for there were good transport facilities in the area and soft water, a necessity in making soft drinks.

1921 exhibition stand, City Hall, Manchester

On 14 December 1912 the name 'VIMTO' was registered as a trade mark in the 'Medicines' class and on 3 February 1913 was registered as a 'beverage for human use, not alcoholic, not aerated, and not medicated'. VIMTO was initially described as a 'Health Tonic', one that 'Keeps You Fit'. Such descriptions were not allowed after the Second World War, but by that time VIMTO was already taken for pleasure and as a thirst quenching drink. J N Nichols and Co were quick to feature VIMTO on the back of their catalogue,

calling it 'Our Speciality'. The retailer added just hot, cold or soda water to the concentrate, but customers were warned 'Beware of Substitutes'.

Noel married his cousin Norah Drennan in 1913. She played a major part in the expansion of the firm, concentrating on the office work which was so essential to its success. The passing of the 1915 Defence of the Realm Act restricted licencing hours, increased excise duty and reduced the strength of alcoholic drinks – these measures were introduced to counter the growing problems of bad time-keeping and public order offences which were affecting the armed forces and industry. Along the way they also provided a boost for the growing mineral water trade!

By 1916 VIMTO was sold to herbalists and temperance bars in North Wales, Yorkshire, Glasgow, Warminster in Wiltshire at the 'Lancashire Temperance Bar', as well as in the North West of England. In 1919 VIMTO was registered as a United Kingdom trade mark in the 'Mineral and Aerated Water' class, as well as being in the 'Medicines' and 'Cordials' classes. That year the first overseas trade mark registration of VIMTO took place in British Guiana, now Guyana. About 1920 concentrated VIMTO

Cinema ad from the twenties (top), and fifties showcard (below). Showcard on the right is from the mid-thirties.

syrup was adapted, so that with the addition of carbonated water, it could be made into a sparkling drink in bulk by bottling agents. Early in the 1920s Richard Goodsir, a friend of Noel Nichols, and the Indian Kiwi boot polish representative, took a few samples of VIMTO concentrate with him to see if he could interest local bottling firms in the drink, and the troops of the North West Regiment provided an immediate market – VIMTO was a taste from home! The name was registered in India in 1924 and advertisements appeared in cinemas and newspapers in both English and local languages and scripts.

By 1926 VIMTO cordial was being bottled by Nichols for general sale, allowing the public to make their own drinks at home. As demand increased the company once more moved to larger premises, to Old Trafford in Manchester. They took over the Britannia Laundry, which had a tall chimney, and very soon the name VIMTO appeared painted on the chimney bricks and a windsock carrying the name flew from a mast. By the end of the decade the company was employing about thirty people.

In 1932 VIMTO cordial was offered to bottlers to sell alongside the sparkling product. They were also encouraged to push the sale of hot VIMTO drinks during winter months when normal sales tended to be lower. In London a publicity campaign announced it was on sale at Selfridges, Fortnum & Masons, and Harrods. VIMTO was now also available as pastilles, as a milk shake syrup, and an ice-cream topping.

In 1939 Noel Nichol's eldest son Peter joined the company straight from school, working in the factory weighing out the herbs, roots and barks for herbalist shops and packing bottles of cordial for export. Throughout the Second World War brand names were not allowed, drinks being sold as 'Speciality Flavour Cordial' which eliminated competition. However VIMTO did continue with small newspaper advertisements with wording such as 'Speed on Victory and the return of VIMTO too'.

After the introduction of the National Health Service, and free prescriptions, herbalists were not in such demand and that side of the business gradually ceased and soft drinks, particularly VIMTO, grew in importance. In 1947 Peter Nichols was made a director and in 1950 John Nichols also joined the company, having obtained a degree in Commerce.

1956 saw the first VIMTO televison advertisement; the 50s and 60s were good years for the soft drinks industry as the new 'teenage' generation

took to them in a big way. Soft drinks were also advertised as part of 'safe-driving' campaigns. In 1961 the company changed its name and became J N Nichols (VIMTO) Ltd, a public company. At the time of flotation the company had sixty employees. In 1964 Noel Nichols became president and technical director and Peter and John became joint managing directors. Noel died in 1966, in his will leaving money to all the long serving employees. His invention of 58 years earlier continued to grow in public esteem and now had a world market. Through widespread and innovative advertising campaigns the name, and taste, of VIMTO became known in millions of homes as 'A Drink for all the Family'.

In 1971 the firm moved to purpose built works and offices in Wythenshawe, South Manchester. The founder's grandsons joined the company, as was tradition, whilst the grand-daughters followed other careers. Peter John, always known as John, came with a degree in Combined Sciences, and his cousin Simon, a chartered accountant with a degree in Business Administration, brought expertise in that area. John is now group managing director and Simon is financial director and company secretary.

In 1999, Vimto production under the name of Vimto Soft Drinks moved to a new factory at Golborne in Greater Manchester. Around 100 people in the United Kingdom are employed directly in the making, marketing and selling of Vimto, with over 395 million litres of finished product sold world-wide each year.

The recipe has varied little since its original formulation. It contains such ingredients as raspberry, blackcurrant, and grape juices, vanilla, capsicum and herb horehound. Natural colours have replaced the artificial ones and vitamin C has also been added. A diet version of sparkling VIMTO was introduced in 1987. The VIMTO concentrate is only made at Golborne, thus ensuring that the secret recipe remains within the company.

The story of Warburtons goes back over a hundred years to the days of large families, days when it was often hard to earn enough money to keep them well fed. George and Thomas Warburton were brothers, members of a family of ten children.

George was born in 1832 and Thomas in 1837. George was a go-ahead young fellow who went out to Australia and when he came back had a thriving cotton waste business in Bolton. Thomas however was physically frail and needed light work, so his brother offered him a job as a doorkeeper and checker. He worked long hours at George's company but always had a secret ambition, to have his own business. When a small grocery shop became available in Blackburn Road in Bolton, Thomas asked George to back his venture, which he did.

Thomas and his wife Ellen opened for business in 1870 and for a time trade was good, but by the middle of the decade it had become difficult to get goods to sell, sales slumped and profits dropped. Ellen, who was a good cook, came up with an idea. She suggested baking some bread and offering it for sale; Thomas was less enthusiastic, for any self-respecting housewife, at that time, made her own. However, they were desperate, and so the next day she did as she had suggested and baked four loaves and six flour cakes. While they were still hot she put them in the window and within the hour they were all sold. The next day she

Top: Rachel Warburton and children outside the shop in Blackburn Road. Below: Henry Warburton becomes Mayor of Bolton, 1930

141

Eatmore still selling well in the fifties

repeated her baking, only this time she doubled the quantities, and again quickly sold out. Within two weeks she was baking full-time.

Soon she could not keep up with demand and the profits were used to buy a bigger coke-fire oven, which allowed her to double her output. The grocery side of the business diminished and the shop was renamed 'Warburtons the Bakers'.

While Thomas's business was recovering and was now doing well, George's business had suffered from falling cotton prices and he had had to close making a heavy loss.

The shop premises belonged to George, but the long hours were badly affecting Thomas' health. George's son, Henry, was keen to learn and was showing a real flair for the bakery trade, so George bought the ovens and the goodwill and father and son began to develop Warburtons. Henry, like his father, had an eye for business and with help from his uncle the trade grew. Often Henry slept on the premises having worked from dawn to dusk. Six days a week he gave it his all, but on Sundays he rested and went to worship at the local Methodist Church. There he eventually met, and fell in love with Rachel Smethurst and in 1888 they married. It is rumoured that they did not even taken a honeymoon for Henry said,

'Bread eaters wait for no man.'

They worked tirelessly together and eventually moved from their small terrace home to a larger house. As the business prospered Henry, now twenty-five and a master baker, bought it from his father for £550.

In April 1891 Rachel and Henry's first child, George, was born – the first of five, who included twins Harry and Billy. As the family grew, so did the business, but it still operated from the bakehouse in the corner shop in Blackburn Road. Soon Henry realised he needed bigger premises so he sold the shop and bakery for £980 and bought the Diamond Jubilee Bakery in Blackbank Street and another shop in Blackburn Road, just up the road from Thomas's original premises. Rachel ran this new shop single handed, although she had also five children to look after. She never complained of all the hard work, but one afternoon Henry took her place and immediately declared that running the home and the shop was bad for her health, and he shut it down!

At the turn of the new century Henry's first employee was his brother-in-law Walt Pendlebury – Walt undertook all the deliveries, using a horse drawn van. A new momentum carried the business forward as two three-decker ovens and a state-of-the-art gas-driven dough mixer were installed; the mixer could handle 280lbs of flour.

As Henry prospered he gained standing in the local community and in 1900 stood as a Liberal candidate for the North Ward of Bolton, winning the seat by fifteen votes – it was the start of 36 years of public service. Warburtons bread was now a familiar sight in many households in the area and some of the profits went towards the building of North House, a new home for himself and his family. Perhaps it was a small reward for all their toil and sacrifice.

Later Henry acquired a disused church in Blackbank Street and converted it into the most modern bakery in Lancashire, filled with all the latest machinery. However, the installation of modern machinery did not affect his insistence on product quality and he personally supervised all stages of production. Competition was fierce, but he drove his workers hard, getting them to start earlier each morning. Even though he had to stand up to the unions over such matters he was well respected, not least for his generosity to the working classes. Rarely did he turn anyone away who was seeking work, even when he had all the staff he needed.

In 1913 he bought a prime piece of land in Hereford Street, called Back o' th' Bank, and drew up plans for a Model Bakery. Unfortunately the outbreak of war meant that many of his staff, including his sons, left to fight for their country and so Henry, his wife and daughter all got involved in bread-making. On the 14th July 1915 Rachel proudly declared the Model Bakery open in front of around 500 guests, including the Mayor of Bolton.

In 1918 Henry had a stroke, but soon his sons were back from the war and played their part in taking the business forward. However, Henry gradually took the helm again and now became involved in a new passion, as a director of First Division Bolton Wanderers Football Club.

Young George and Billy toured America looking at both baking and marketing – they were impressed by the slogans the bakers used, such as 'The Loaf That Stopped Mother Baking'. British housewives were not yet ready for such ideas, but George was keen to give his product 'added value' and created the 'Eatmore' concept, a tasty malted loaf that kept well.

In 1930 Henry Warburton became Mayor of Bolton, Chairman of Bolton Wanderers, and a member of Bolton Rotary Club; all gave him great opportunities to serve the community.

However, the 1930s were tough years for the business. Warburtons had been the first to introduce automatic wrapping of loaves, but in other ways they were slipping behind. With motorised transport they could deliver further and further from Bolton, and Billy now promoted the idea of their own retail shops, to which bread and cakes were delivered fresh from the bakery. In 1936 Henry died, aged 71. It was the end of an era, but much re-equipping needed to be done, and they had to go to the bank for loans to do so. They transferred the company's wholesale cake operation to larger premises at Bakewell Works in Derby Street – new machinery included a versatile Swiss roll oven; confectionery was now an increasingly important

part of the business.

After the Second World War expansion continued – Warburtons diversified their range of products and also made significant acquisitions, including Imperial bakeries, the manufacturers of Soreen Malt loaf. Around 1965 they were operating five bakeries and running 38 confectionery shops. Unfortunately deaths in 1966 were to rob the company of the twin brothers, Harry and Billy Warburton. They had played a major role in the company's expansion, but the founder's policy of baking the best possible bread continued. In the late 1960s the famous Blackpool Milk loaf was introduced and became an instant hit with children and the elderly.

In the 1970s the company purchased Allans of Bolton and entered the savoury pie business, trading as Peter Hunt's. It was a decade which saw bread consumption fall and the sale of packaged cakes also decline dramatically. However, with the company's usual determination they redoubled their efforts to improve efficiency and retain their market share.

In 1976 Warburtons celebrated their centenary and were honoured to be visited by Her Royal Highness, The Princess Alexandra. They still had trading problems as supermarkets bought bread from the larger bakers at low prices, which enabled them to use bread as a loss leader. The company refused to sacrifice standards and continued to import their traditional Canadian and

North American bread flours. In 1978 Spillers, one of their largest rivals, ceased bread production and this enabled Warburton's share of the market to grow once again.

A new £3 million bakery was opened in Burnley in 1981 and later in the decade a bakery was opened at Newburn in the north east. In 1990 Warburtons acquired Sayers of Liverpool, another well known family business, which gave them a bigger presence in the retail bakery market.

In 1988 the fourth generation members of the Warburton family stepped down from management of the company and were succeeded by Jim Speak who had joined the company as an engineer in 1954 and risen to become chairman.

After three years at the helm it was now time for the fifth generation of the family to take over and lead the company into the next millennium. Ross, grandson of Billy Warburton, became chairman, and cousins Jonathon and Brett, grandsons of the other twin, Harry Warburton, became joint managing directors.

In 1991 they sold the wholesale cake bakery in Bolton to Northern Foods and opened a new distribution depot in Alfreton, Derbyshire, as part of a strategy towards Warburtons becoming recognised nationally and throughout Europe. Now each week Warburtons' products, particularly bread and its Soreen Fruity Malt Loaf, are exported into Belgium, France, Spain, and the Balearic and Canary Islands.

In 1995 a new bakery was built in Eastwood, Nottingham and in 1998 Warburtons eighth bread bakery was opened in Bellshill near Glasgow.

It is well over a century since Ellen Warburton baked her first loaf to offer for sale – today Warburtons is the United Kingdom's leading independent bakery group, still looking to offer quality foods as Thomas and Ellen did in the 1870s.